The *Rice* COOKBOOK

The *Rice*
COOKBOOK

Anne Dettmer & Victoria Lloyd-Davies

TED SMART

WITH THE SUPPORT OF THE RICE BUREAU

rice
BUREAU

LONDON

Specially produced for Ted Smart,
Guardian House, Borough Road,
Godalming, Surrey GU7 2AE

All correspondence concerning the content of this volume should
be addressed to Salamander Books Ltd, 129–137 York Way,
London N7 9 LG, United Kingdom.

CREDITS

AUTHORS: *Anne Dettmer and Victoria Lloyd-Davies*
EDITOR: *Lisa Dyer*
DESIGNER: *Rachel Griffin*
PHOTOGRAPHER: *Simon Butcher*
STYLIST: *Marian Price*
COPY EDITOR: *Hilaire Walden*
FILM: *Flairplan Photo-typesetting Ltd, England*
COLOUR SEPARATION: *P&W Graphics Pte Ltd, Singapore*

Printed in Singapore

When making any of the recipes in this book, you should follow either the metric or
the imperial measures, as these are not interchangeable.

As seasoning is a matter of taste, salt and pepper have not
been listed in the ingredients.

Contents

AUTHORS' INTRODUCTION

Rice appears in an assortment of shapes and sizes, ranging from short and tubby, through gently rounded, to long and slender. It is this vast array of different rice types and their individual characteristics that add interest and variety to our culinary experiences.

The Latin term for rice is *Oryza sativa*, a name used to describe a cereal that is thought to have, at the very least, 40,000 strains within its botanical family. Although it is not possible to cover each of these variants in this book, the rice types obtainable in today's supermarkets and specialist shops have been included.

Each rice type behaves differently when cooked, therefore choosing the correct rice when preparing a specific dish is essential to achieve the required result. Some people who imagine they lack the skill to cook rice may have inadvertently used the wrong rice. Once armed with the knowledge of marrying rice types to cooking characteristics, the most inexperienced cook can prepare rice dishes with the flair of an accomplished chef. To dispel any mystique surrounding cooking rice, a cooking chart has been included on page 14, but do remember the cooking times are a guideline only.

To explore the world of rice is an exciting journey. Grown on every continent of the world except Antarctica, rice has inspired some of the finest culinary creations from around the globe. You will find many of these dishes within this collection of recipes, such as the classic and elegant risottos of Italy, the robust and fiery American Cajun and Creole dishes, the skilfully spiced Middle Eastern and South-east Asian recipes, the colourful creations of Spain and the precisely prepared delicacies of Japan. You will discover not only familiar dishes which you may have enjoyed in ethnic restaurants or whilst travelling abroad, but also those which may surprise you by their ingenious treatment of rice.

There are recipes to suit every occasion, whether formal or informal entertaining, quick suppers and family meals, snacks, starters, salads or puddings. Many of the recipes in this book are suitable for vegetarians. And, as all rice is gluten-free, coeliacs can safely eat it, so adding interest to a diet which must avoid products that contain the protein gluten.

One of the joys of rice is that rice is always on hand when you need it. Not restricted by seasonal availability, rice will keep in the kitchen cupboard for some time before its 'best before' date expires. This is an advantage if you wish to try a recipe using a rice type which is unfamiliar to you, as you will not have to worry about wasting part of the packet, and you can try the rice again at a later date. With this in mind, it is worth experimenting with many varieties of rice. Remember too that there is no laborious peeling or preparation to be done and that most rice approximately trebles in size when cooked. This is particularly beneficial when storage space is at a premium, such as on camping or caravanning holidays.

For those who need meals quickly, some recipes based on convenience rice, such as canned or frozen rice, are included. These rices can make all the difference when time is tight and water in quantity is difficult to obtain. With its amazing versatility in recipes and in type, its healthy attributes and simplicity in cooking, rice is a truly splendid and special grain, and one to sample time and time again.

Victoria Lloyd-Davies

THE HISTORY OF RICE

To pin-point exactly when mankind first realised that the rice plant was a food source and began its cultivation is impossible. Many historians believe that rice was grown as far back as 5000 years BC.

Archaeologists excavating in India discovered rice which, they were convinced, could be dated to 4530 BC. However, the first recorded mention originates from China in 2800 BC. The Chinese emperor, Shen Nung, realised the importance of rice to his people and to honour the grain he established annual rice ceremonies to be held at sowing time, with the emperor scattering the first seeds. Most likely, similar ceremonies took place throughout China with local dignitaries deputising for the emperor. Nowadays, the Chinese celebrate rice by specifically dedicating one of the days in the New Year festivities to it.

Although we can not identify China, India or Thailand as being the home of the rice plant (indeed it may have been native to all), we can be more certain of how rice was introduced to Europe and the Americas. For that we have to thank the traveller, whether explorer, soldier, merchant or pilgrim, who took with them seeds of the crops that grew in their home or foreign lands.

Not all seeds could be transplanted successfully, however. Great Britain has never been able to cultivate rice due to adverse climatic conditions. The rice plant requires immense quantities of rainfall in its early days, followed by a long and uninterrupted season of hot, dry weather. For this reason, farmers must find ways to either flood the fields or drain the water from them at crucial periods.

In the West, parts of America and certain regions of Europe, such as Italy and Spain, are able to provide the correct climate thereby giving rise to a thriving rice industry. Some historians believe that rice travelled to America in 1694 in a British ship bound for Madagascar.

Blown off course into the safe harbour of Charleston, South Carolina, friendly colonists helped the crew repair their ships. To show his gratitude, the ship's captain, James Thurber, presented Henry Woodward with a quantity of rice seed.

Some years later, the British unfortunately blotted their copybook in relation to the rice industry they had probably initiated. During the American Revolution, they occupied the Charleston area and sent home the entire quantity of harvested rice, failing to leave any seed for the following year's crop.

The American rice industry survived this set-back and cultivation continued, thanks to President Thomas Jefferson, who broke an Italian law by smuggling rice seed out of Italy during a diplomatic mission in the late 18th century. The rice industry then transplanted itself from the Carolinas to the southern states surrounding the Mississippi basin.

Rice is so fundamentally important to various cultures that it is often directly associated with prosperity, and much folklore and legend surrounds the grain. In many cultures and societies, rice is integrated directly into religious belief. In Japan rice enjoys the patronage of its own god, Inari, and in Indonesia its own goddess, the Dewie Srie.

Rice is also linked to fertility and for this reason the custom of throwing rice at newly wedded couples exists. In India, rice is always the first food offered by a new bride to her husband, to ensure fertility in the marriage, and children are given rice as their first solid food. And, according to Louisiana folklore, the test of a true Cajun is whether he can calculate the precise quantity of gravy needed to accompany a crop of rice growing in a field. How easy to see that from its early beginnings to the present day, rice continues to play an integral role in sustaining both the world's appetites and cultural traditions.

Only fairly recently have major supermarkets begun to sell a substantial range of different rice types. With few exceptions, those described in this book can be purchased alongside your regular shopping needs, although you may have to buy one or two of the more unusual rices from specialist shops.

The various types of rice behave differently when cooked mainly because of variations in the ratio of the starches, amylose and amylopectin they contain. If amylopectin is predominant, as it is in short and medium grain rice, the grains have a greater tendency to cling together when cooked, whereas if amylopectin is low and amylose high, as in long grain rice, each cooked rice grain is dry and fluffy and remains separate.

Grains are classified by their length, and, on the whole, the longer the grain in relation to its width the more separate the grains will remain on cooking. There are always exceptions however, such as jasmine rice, so although length is a good general guide, the definitions which follow should be consulted before making a definitive judgement based on grain length.

Although the individual characteristics for each rice type governs their suitability for the preparation of specific dishes, there is one type that is labelled as long grain and regarded by many as all purpose. Using long grain rice for all dishes may indeed supply satisfactory results, but may not always conform to the ethnic correctness of the resulting dish. Nevertheless, knowing when long grain rice can be substituted for a speciality variety is useful, so suggested substitutions have been included where appropriate throughout the book.

LONG GRAIN OR ALL-PURPOSE RICE

The long grain rices are exported mainly from the USA, Italy, Spain, Surinam, Guyana and Thailand. At one time long grain rice was exported from India and was called Patna after the district in which it grew. The majority of long grain rice imported into Britain originates from America.

Long grain rice has a slim grain that is four to five times as long as it is wide. Harvested straight from the field, long grain is known as 'rough' or 'paddy' rice but undergoes different milling techniques to result in the following four choices.

REGULAR LONG GRAIN WHITE RICE The husk and bran layers are removed in milling to produce a white grain. When cooked, the grain tends to separate and fluff, retaining a minute cling. To avoid too much cling, ensure this rice is not over-cooked.

This rice has a subtle flavour which is complementary to either a richly flavoured or a delicate dish, so it is enormously versatile and can be used for numerous international dishes. This rice is ideal for American, Mexican, Spanish (except for paella) and Caribbean recipes and it is particularly good for Chinese dishes, especially if chopsticks are to be used. Also try long grain white rice for stuffings.

REGULAR LONG GRAIN BROWN RICE Also known as wholegrain rice, this type undergoes only minor milling, sufficient to remove the husk, but leave the bran layer intact. The flavour is distinctly nutty and the retention of the bran layer ensures higher fibre, vitamin and mineral content than is found in white rice.

The grains remain separate when cooked, as with long grain white rice, but they take longer to soften. The cooked grains have a chewy texture which many people enjoy. Long grain brown rice can be used to prepare any of the dishes referred to above, but is particularly suited to wholefood styles of cooking.

EASY-COOK LONG GRAIN WHITE RICE Sometimes known as parboiled, converted or pre-fluffed, this type is the ideal choice for the novice rice cook. Unlike regular long grain white rice, which is milled direct from the field, easy-cook long grain rice is steamed under pressure first, whilst still intact, which hardens the grain making it virtually impossible to over-cook. Another benefit is that

Regular Long Grain White

Regular Long Grain Brown

Easy-Cook Long Grain White

Easy-Cook Long Grain Brown

the process captures much of the natural vitamin and mineral content present in the outer layers and pushes these vitamins and minerals into the grain itself, before the layers are discarded in the milling which follows. Although golden in colour when raw, easy-cook long grain white rice turns white on cooking and the grains remain completely separate. It has a slightly fuller flavour than regular white rice but can be used in the same ways, although is not quite as good for Chinese dishes or stuffings. It is particularly well suited to rice salads and stir fries.

EASY-COOK LONG GRAIN BROWN RICE This type of long grain is ideal for both the novice cook and those who find regular brown rice slightly too chewy. Not only is it lighter than regular brown rice but takes less time to cook. Again, easy-cook long grain brown rice suits wholefood and vegetarian dishes or recipes where its nutty taste will be appreciated.

SPECIALITY RICES

These rice types include aromatics, risotto, glutinous and pudding rice, among others, and often have a specific ethnic use. Grown, cooked and eaten, more often than not, at the same location, these rices have been central to various geographical regions' survival, but now increased trade between countries has expanded availability and choice in many markets. Some countries, however, still consume all the rice they grow. Improved farming practices may well yield new types appearing in the shops in the years to come.

THE AROMATICS The first class of rice which is termed speciality is aromatic rice. This contains a natural ingredient known as 2-acetyl 1-pyroline, which is responsible for the fragrant taste and aroma. As with wines, the fragrance quality of aromatic rice can differ from one year's harvest to another. The finest aromatic rices are also aged to bring out the aromatic strength.

Basmati White

Basmati Easy-Cook White

Basmati Brown

American Basmati White

Jasmine

American Jasmine White

American Jasmine Brown

Wild Pecan

Basmati Rice: An extremely slender, long grain, aromatic rice with a perfumed taste and aroma. Grown in India and Pakistan, mainly around the foothills of the Himalayas, it is used in Indian cuisine.

Basmati white is the one most commonly served in Indian restaurants. The grains are separate and fluffy on cooking. Indian cooks often prepare basmati with other spices to enhance the grain's aromatic properties. The easy-cook variety is a relatively recent introduction for those who appreciate the advantages of the easy-cook process. Basmati brown rice is also quite a new introduction and has a higher fibre content and even stronger aroma than ordinary basmati white.

Jasmine Rice: Also known as Thai fragrant rice, this rice originates from Thailand. Although the length and slimness of the grains suggest they remain separate on cooking, jasmine rice does become soft and slightly sticky when cooked. Its aroma is less pronounced than that of a basmati rice. It is used mainly in South-east Asian cooking, but can also be used for Chinese dishes.

American Aromatics: The American rice industry has developed a series of aromatic rices to mimic the fragrance of both basmati and jasmine rice. Available in either brown, white or mid-way between the two, called micromill, the grains look like a long grain rice. There are several varieties, but they are generally not available in Great Britain. However some speciality shops may carry American basmati, American jasmine, Wild Pecan or Popcorn rice. Another unusual aromatic is Wehani which is russet red in colour.

RISOTTO RICE Risotto is a category of rice which is used specifically to make the classic Italian risotto dish, and includes several types, such as Arborio and Carnaroli. Whereas most rices can absorb around three times their weight in liquid, a risotto rice can absorb up to five times. It is a medium grain rice and during cooking starch is released, encouraging the grains to cling together. Brown easy-cook risotto rice is also available.

American Popcorn White

American Popcorn Brown

Wehani

Risotto (Arborio)

BAHIA RICE A medium-grained rice originating from Spain, bahia rice is used to make the Spanish national dish, paella. As bahai is not as widely available as risotto, the latter can be substituted for it in recipes.

GLUTINOUS RICE A category of rice which is also know as sweet, sticky or waxy rice, and types available include Japanese, Chinese and Thai.

Japanese Glutinous Rice: This rice has a round pearl-like grain which becomes sticky on cooking and has a slightly sweet taste. It is used by Japanese cooks to make sushi, which is a mixture of rice, vinegar and sugar. The preparation can be laborious as the rice has to be fanned with a wooden paddle as it cools. Sushi is traditionally served wrapped in nori, or omelette strips.

Chinese Glutinous Rice: Chalkier in colour than Japanese glutinous rice, this rice is used mainly in the preparation of stuffings and for puddings.

Thai Glutinous Rice: This rice is available in both white and black grains, both of which are popular for Thai puddings. The grains are not as round in shape as the Japanese and Chinese glutinous rice grains.

PUDDING RICE Originally called Carolina rice due to its early source in America, but now referred to as either pudding or short grain rice and imported mainly from Italy. The grains, which are tubby and chalky white in colour, stick together when cooked. Used mainly to make traditional rice puddings, pudding rice is unsuitable for savoury dishes where separate grains are desired. Both white and brown rices are available.

WILD RICE This is not actually a rice at all, but an aquatic grass that grows wild along the waterways of North America. Wild rice was the traditional food of American Indians who harvested it from canoes. The plant would be hit with the paddle and if the grain was ripe it would fall into the canoe. Any grain falling back into the water germinated to produce the next crop.

Risotto Carnaroli

Easy-Cook Risotto Brown

Bahia

Japanese Glutinous

Chinese Glutinous

Thai Black Glutinous

Pudding Rice

Wild Rice

Wild rice is very dark in colour, ranging from brown to black and the grain is extremely long. It is prized as a gourmet rice and can certainly be pricey. Many food companies provide wild rice mixes, blending wild rice with either a long grain or a basmati.

CONVENIENCE RICES

Cooking rice is neither laborious nor time intensive, although there are days when short cuts are highly desirable. To help with preparing meals quickly, commercially prepared rice is worth keeping in the store-cupboard or freezer. Be sure to read the cooking instructions before using.

FROZEN RICE Cooked and then frozen, this convenience rice is readily available in supermarket freezer cabinets. Packed in both multi-serving and single-portion sachets, it suits either the microwave or conventional reheating. Frozen rice is normally ready to serve in around three minutes. Frozen rice mixed with vegetables is also available.

CANNED RICE Also ready-cooked, canned rice responds well to both microwave and conventional reheating, and is available in white and brown, generally in 277 g (9.7 oz) cans. Recent introductions include ethnic style mixes. Remember to remove the rice from the can before reheating.

QUICK OR FAST-COOK RICE This rice has been cooked and dried, and, although not as instant as either frozen or canned rice, it is speedier to cook than a raw rice as it is normally ready in ten minutes. It is often available packed in portion-controlled sachets.

BOIL-IN-THE-BAG RICE This rice is conveniently contained in portion packs so it is easy to calculate the required amounts. However, the cooking time is not reduced. Both brown and white varieties are available.

DRY RICE MIXES There is now a range of dry rice mixes to chose from, spanning those which are lightly flavoured with herbs and spices to those mixed with vegetables. Rice mixes are usually packed in sachets and make a useful accompaniment to many meals.

RICE PRODUCTS

Rice can be milled to produce flakes, flour, bran and ground rice which are used in baking, puddings and food manufacturing. Some well-known breakfast cereals are made with rice, and rice cakes, similar to rusks, are growing in popularity. Suitable for sweet and savoury toppings, rice cakes are very low in calories. A coeliac's diet can be supplemented by rice shapes to provide an alternative to wheat pasta, and rice bread and biscuits can be purchased as well. Oriental rice noodles, edible rice paper and savoury rice crackers are widely available. Rice is brewed to make wine, beer, sake and vinegar.

RICE NUTRITION

Rice is an extremely healthy food for a number of reasons. Rice is a complex carbohydrate, which means that it contains starch and fibre whereas a simple carbohydrate is a sugar. Simple carbohydrates are quickly digested and provide a fast energy boost, but one which is not sustained. However complex carbohydrates are digested much more slowly, allowing the body to utilise the energy released over a longer period which is nutritionally more efficient.

Rice has a very low sodium content and contains useful quantities of potassium, the B vitamins, thiamin and niacin. An average portion of rice (50 g/2 oz raw or 175 g/6 oz cooked) provides about 11% of the adult estimated average daily requirement of protein. One portion also has only 245 kcal. Those looking to reduce their fat and cholesterol intake can turn to rice because it contains virtually no fat and no cholesterol.

Rice is also gluten-free, so suitable for coeliacs, and it is easily digested, and therefore a wonderful food for the

LEFT: *Many rice products are available on the market, such as rice flakes, flour, bran, breakfast cereal, rice cakes and biscuits, pasta and noodles, and vinegar, beer and sake.*

very young and the elderly. Rice is suitable for vegetarians and vegans, with brown rice in particular complementing vegetarian and vegan dishes.

STORING RICE

Rice will keep for a considerable time, although it is wise to observe the 'best before' date shown on the packet. Unopened packets should be stored in a cool, dry cupboard, but once opened any unused rice should be transferred to an air-tight container.

Cool leftover cooked rice quickly, then cover it to prevent drying out or the absorption of smells and flavours from other foods, and either keep the rice in the refrigerator for up to 24 hours (providing the temperature is 5°C or below) or divide it into portions and freeze it. Follow the appropriate marking on your freezer for storage times.

COOKING RICE

There are four main methods of cooking rice, and which to choose is a matter of personal choice. However, in some recipes, such as in Herbed Lemon Rice on page 40, a specific method should be followed. Please refer to the chart for recommended quantities and times, and add salt to taste.

ABSORPTION In this method a precise measure of cold liquid is added to a precise quantity of rice, so that by the end of the cooking, when the rice is tender, all the liquid will have been absorbed.

Put 250 g (9 oz) of rice and the recommended amount of cold water into a saucepan. Bring to the boil and stir once. Lower heat to a gentle simmer, cover the pan with a tight-fitting lid, and cook for the recommended time until the rice is tender and the liquid absorbed. Take the rice out of the pan, and transfer to a serving dish.

TYPES OF RICE	QUANTITY OF RICE FOR ALL METHODS	QUANTITY OF WATER FOR ABSORPTION METHOD	COOKING TIMES FOR HOB FOR ALL METHODS	COOKING TIMES FOR Oven (180°C/ 350°F/GAS MARK 4)	MICROWAVE ABSORPTION METHOD COOKING TIMES, PLUS 10 MINUTES STANDING. 650 WATT FULL POWER
Regular long grain white	250 g (9 oz)	500 ml (18 fl oz)	12 minutes	40 minutes	8 minutes
Easy-cook long grain white	250 g (9 oz)	550 ml (19 fl oz)	15 minutes	45 minutes	10 minutes
Basmati white	250 g (9 oz)	450 ml (3/4 pint)	10 minutes	35 minutes	6 minutes
Easy-cook basmati white	250 g (9 oz)	600 ml (1 pint)	12 minutes	40 minutes	7 minutes
Regular long grain brown	250 g (9 oz)	625 ml (21 fl oz)	35 minutes	1 hour 15 minutes	25 minutes
Easy-cook long grain brown	250 g (9 oz)	650 ml (23 fl oz)	30 minutes	1 hour 10 minutes	18 minutes
Basmati brown	250 g (9 oz)	600 ml (1 pint)	25 minutes	50 minutes	16 minutes
Jasmine	250 g (9 oz)	450 ml (3/4 pint)	10 minutes	35 minutes	6 minutes
Wild	250 g (9 oz)	750 ml (26 fl oz)	45 minutes	1 hour 40 minutes	38 minutes
Risotto (medium grain)	250 g (9 oz)	1 litre (13/4 pints)	20 minutes	–	–
Glutinous	250 g (9 oz)	450 ml (3/4 pint)	15 minutes	–	–
Pudding (short grain)	50 g (2 oz)	600 ml (1 pint) (milk)	40 minutes	2 hours (150°C/ 300°F/Gas mark 1)	8 minutes + 40 minutes on defrost
Convenience rices	Check packet instructions				

FREE SIMMER In this method the rice is added to a much larger volume of boiling liquid, then excess liquid is drained off at the end of the cooking time. Put 250 g (9 oz) of rice and 1.4 litres (2¼ pints) boiling water into a large saucepan. Bring back to the boil and simmer, uncovered, for the recommended time until rice is tender. Drain in a sieve. Rinse with more boiling water. Drain and serve.

MICROWAVE This is a convenient method as the rice can be cooked and served in the same dish. However, the rice takes as long to cook as for other methods because it must have a 'standing' time of 10 minutes.

Put 250 g (9 oz) rice and the recommended amount of boiling water into a deep glass bowl or deep microwave container. Stir once. Cover and microwave on full power for the recommended time. Remove bowl from the microwave and leave to stand for 10 minutes before serving - it will continue to cook and absorb liquid after you remove it from the microwave. You may need to reduce the liquid quantity by 50 ml (2 fl oz) if you have a sealed container that reduces the evaporation of the liquid.

COMBINATION METHOD If you wish to cook rice before cooking the rest of the dish, cook rice either by absorption or free simmer until just tender. Cool in a sieve under cold running water. Drain thoroughly and refrigerate. When required, reheat rice in a covered glass bowl or microwave container on full power for approximately 4 minutes.

Alternatively, an electrical rice cooker or rice steamer may be used. These are now widely available from several manufacturers, and are particularly advantageous if you eat rice often or cook in large quantities.

REHEATING RICE

Rice can be reheated in many ways. Place rice in a covered colander over a saucepan of simmering water, and shake the pan frequently until the rice is hot throughout. Alternatively, rice can be added to a saucepan of boiling water, boiled for 2-3 minutes then drained. Or, spread the rice in a well-buttered baking tin, cover with foil, and place in a preheated oven at 190°C (375°F/Gas mark 5) for about 30 minutes. Other options are to preheat a little oil in a pan and stir-fry the rice, or place the rice in a microwave-proof bowl with a little water and cook in the microwave for a few minutes until piping hot. Do ensure the rice is thoroughly heated.

HINTS AND TIPS

- Rice trebles in size when cooked. Allow at least 50 g (2 oz) uncooked rice per person.

- Rinse rice to remove starch before cooking, not after cooking. It is not necessary to rinse any all-purpose long grain rice and never rinse or soak risotto rice.

- To rinse basmati, jasmine, glutinous and pudding rice, place dry rice into a deep bowl. Fill the bowl with cold water and swirl the rice around with your hand. Allow the grains to settle in the bottom of the bowl. Then carefully tip the bowl so that the water drains out, leaving the grains. Repeat four to six times until the water runs clear.

- Soaking rice reduces its cooking time. To soak, place dry or rinsed rice into a deep bowl, fill it with cold water and leave for 30 minutes. Drain well through a sieve, then proceed as usual.

- As a general rule, use long grain rice for savoury dishes, medium grain for risottos and short grain for puddings. Regular milled long grain rice is best for stuffings, but use easy-cook in stir fries and salads when you want every grain to be separate.

- If you want separate grains, choose all-purpose long grain or basmati rices. Risotto, jasmine and glutinous rices always cling together and should never be rinsed after cooking.

- Glutinous rice needs special care - always use a large pan and simmer at the lowest possible heat. Never lift the lid off the pan. Leave rice in the pan for 10 minutes after cooking.

- Always add boiling water or stock to rice when making a risotto or cooking in the microwave. If possible, use home-made stocks, such as vegetable water or liquid from simmered chicken bones.

- To cool rice quickly, put it in a sieve over a bowl, then gently prod, at intervals, with the handle of a wooden spoon. This will release steam and heat.

- For fried rice, cook the rice and refrigerate it for two hours before needed so that most of the moisture has evaporated. Then stir fry in very hot oil to avoid the rice absorbing the fat.

- Always fill rice pans with cold water and leave them to soak while you eat to facilitate washing the pans.

- Fluff up rice with a fork just before serving.

- Rice absorbs flavours so cook it with meat, chicken and vegetable stocks, fruit juices and milk. White rice also absorbs colour from saffron, turmeric and curry spices.

- To settle upset stomachs, boil rice, without rinsing it first, then strain the starchy liquid into a jug. Then allow to cool before drinking the rice water.

SOUPS & STARTERS

The use of rice is not confined to main courses and puddings; indeed, rice occurs in numerous guises to make soups and starters from around the world, one of the most unusual being lontong - small cubes of cooked, cooled rice, often used in recipes from the Far East.

RICE & CHEESE BALLS WITH TOMATO SAUCE

25 g (1 oz) UNSALTED BUTTER
125 g (4 oz) BROWN EASY-COOK RISOTTO RICE
450 ml (3/4 pint) VEGETABLE STOCK
45 ml (3 tbsp) FLOUR
1 or 2 FRESH GREEN CHILLIES, SEEDED AND FINELY CHOPPED
2 pinches BICARBONATE OF SODA
50 g (2 oz) CHEDDAR CHEESE, GRATED
2.5 ml (1/2 tsp) ENGLISH MUSTARD POWDER
1 (size 4) EGG, BEATEN
50 g (2 oz) FRESH BROWN BREADCRUMBS

Tomato Sauce
15 ml (1 tbsp) OLIVE OIL
3 SHALLOTS, FINELY CHOPPED
6 TOMATOES, SKINNED AND ROUGHLY CHOPPED
3 SUN-DRIED TOMATOES, FINELY CHOPPED
3 LARGE FRESH BASIL LEAVES, CHOPPED

Heat the butter in a saucepan. Add the rice and cook, stirring, for 2 minutes. Add the stock, bring to the boil and stir. Cover and simmer for 25 minutes until the liquid has been absorbed. Stir in the flour, chillies, bicarbonate of soda, cheese and mustard. Cool.

Meanwhile, make the sauce. Heat the oil in a saucepan and fry the shallots for 2 minutes. Add the fresh and dried tomatoes and simmer gently for 10 minutes. Stir in the basil, remove from the heat and cover to keep warm.

Heat a deep-fat fryer half-filled with oil to 180°C (350°F). With floured hands, shape the mixture into 30 walnut-sized balls. Dip each ball in beaten egg, then coat in breadcrumbs. Deep fry, six at a time, for 2 minutes until golden. Drain on paper towels. Reheat sauce gently, if necessary, and serve with the hot balls.   SERVES 6

CALIFORNIA COMPANY

250 g (9 oz) LONG GRAIN WHITE RICE
4 WHOLE CANNED PIMENTOS, CHOPPED
4 SMALL FRESH GREEN CHILLIES, SEEDED AND THINLY SLICED
6 (size 4) EGGS
125 ml (4.5 fl oz) MILK
125 g (4 oz) CHEDDAR CHEESE, GRATED

Preheat the oven to 180°C (350°F/Gas mark 4). Grease a 22.5 x 30 cm (9 x 12 inch) baking tin. Cook the rice as directed on page 14. Cool, then mix with the pimentos and chillies, reserving a little. Transfer to the tin. Whisk the eggs into the milk and pour over the rice. Sprinkle on cheese. Decorate with pimentos and chillies. Bake for 35-40 minutes until set.   MAKES 12

TOP: RICE & CHEESE BALLS   BOTTOM: CALIFORNIA COMPANY

ORIENTAL LETTUCE CUPS

1 ROUND LETTUCE

50 g (2 oz) LEAN PORK MEAT, CHOPPED INTO SMALL PIECES

50 g (2 oz) PEELED COOKED PRAWNS

5 ml (1 tsp) FRESHLY GRATED ROOT GINGER

2.5 ml (1/2 tsp) CORNFLOUR

30 ml (2 tbsp) SWEET SHERRY

15 ml (1 tbsp) SOY SAUCE

50 g (2 oz) LONG GRAIN WHITE RICE

25 g (1 oz) PINE KERNELS

15 ml (1 tbsp) OIL

1/2 SMALL RED PEPPER, SEEDED AND CHOPPED

4 SPRING ONIONS, TRIMMED AND CHOPPED

1/2 x 198 g (7 oz) CAN WATER CHESTNUTS, DRAINED AND QUARTERED

15 ml (1 tbsp) OYSTER SAUCE

Separate the lettuce leaves and arrange in twos or threes to make cup-shapes. Put pork and prawns in a bowl and add ginger, cornflour, 10 ml (2 tsp) sherry and 5 ml (1 tsp) soy sauce and mix. Set aside.

Cook the rice as directed on page 14. Toast the pine kernels under the grill until lightly browned.

Heat the oil in a wok or large frying pan and stir-fry the pork and prawn mixture for 2 minutes, until the pork is cooked through. Add the pepper and spring onions and continue stir-frying for a further 2 minutes. Add pine kernels, water chestnuts, remaining sherry and soy sauce, and oyster sauce. Bring to the boil and cook for 1 minute. Spoon a little of the rice into the lettuce leaf cups and top with the mixture.   SERVES 4

DOLMADES

30 ml (2 tbsp) OLIVE OIL

1 ONION, FINELY CHOPPED

1 CLOVE GARLIC, CRUSHED

75 g (3 oz) LONG GRAIN WHITE RICE

175 g (6 oz) MINCED PORK

175 ml (6 fl oz) WATER

24 FRESH VINE LEAVES, or *227 g (8 oz)* PACKET VINE LEAVES IN BRINE, DRAINED

15 ml (1 tbsp) LEMON JUICE

125 ml (1/4 pint) TOMATO JUICE

142 ml (1/4 pint) SOURED CREAM

Heat the oil and fry the onion and garlic until tender. Add the rice and pork and cook for 5 minutes. Pour on the water and cook by the absorption method, page 13. Tip into a bowl and cool. Preheat oven to 180°C (350°F/Gas mark 4).

Blanch the fresh vine leaves for 1 minute. If using preserved vine leaves, follow the packet instructions. Drain on paper towels and lay dull-side upwards. Add the lemon juice to the rice mixture. Place a dessertspoonful of rice in the centre of each vine leaf, fold and roll up tightly. Pack tightly in a casserole, then pour on the tomato juice. Cover and bake for 45 minutes. Pour tomato juices into a pan and boil to thicken slightly. Remove from the heat and stir in the soured cream. Pour the sauce around the warm vine leaves.   MAKES 20-24

TOP: DOLMADES   BOTTOM: ORIENTAL LETTUCE CUPS

ROLLED SUSHI

4 SHEETS OF DRIED NORI SEAWEED

Vinegared Rice

120 ml (8 tbsp) SUGAR

120 ml (8 tbsp) RICE VINEGAR

2.5 ml (1/2 tsp) SALT

450 g (1 lb) GLUTINOUS WHITE RICE

625 ml (21 fl oz) WATER

Filling

4 DRIED SHIITAKE MUSHROOMS, SOAKED IN HOT WATER FOR *30* MINUTES

40 ml (2 tbsp plus 2 tsp) SOY SAUCE

20 ml (1 tbsp plus 1 tsp) WATER

5 ml (1 tsp) OIL

1 (size 4) EGG, BEATEN

5 ml (1 tsp) WASABI (OR ENGLISH MUSTARD POWDER)

50 g (2 oz) FRESH SALMON FILLET, CUT INTO 0.5 CM (1/4 INCH) THICK STRIPS

1/3 CUCUMBER, CUT INTO THIN STRIPS

To Serve

WASABI

SOY SAUCE

To prepare the rice, dissolve the sugar in the rice vinegar over a gentle heat. Add the salt then set aside. Wash the rice in several changes of water until the water is no longer milky. Leave the rice to drain for 1 hour. Put the rice and water in a saucepan. Cover the pan with foil, then a tight-fitting lid. Bring to the boil, then turn the heat to very low and cook for 20 minutes. Increase the heat to high for 3 seconds, then turn it off. Leave, covered, for 15 minutes. Do not remove the lid at any stage.

Tip the rice on to a large baking tray, then pour over the vinegar. Fan the rice with a rolled magazine or lid, while mixing the rice gently with a dampened wooden paddle or spoon. Continue until the rice is at room temperature. Place the rice in a covered bowl and set aside in a cool place.

Meanwhile, drain the mushrooms, discard the hard stems, then cut into thin strips. Cook the mushrooms over a gentle heat with 30 ml (2 tbsp) of the soy sauce and 15 ml (1 tbsp) water for 5 minutes.

Heat the oil in a small omelette pan. Beat the egg with the remaining water, then pour into the pan to cover the base evenly. Using a fork or spatula, lift the edges of the omelette, allowing the liquid to flow on to the pan. Continue until the omelette is nearly set. Remove from the pan and cool. Then roll up and cut into 0.5 cm (1/4 inch) strips. Cover and set aside. Mix the wasabi and remaining soy sauce in a small dish.

Toast the nori, if necessary, by holding a sheet in a pair of tongs and waving it over a medium flame. The nori becomes paler in colour and fragrant. Place one nori on a sudare (bamboo mat) or on a clean tea towel. Using a slightly wet hand, take one-quarter of the rice and spread evenly over the nori. Place one-quarter of the salmon strips along the centre of the rice. Brush with a little of the wasabi mixture. Arrange one-quarter each of the cucumber strips, omelette and mushrooms on top and to the side, in neat rows, keeping as close to the centre as possible.

Moisten the nori edges with water. Using the sudare mat or towel to help, carefully roll up the sushi, keeping the filling in place with your fingers, if necessary. Cut into six equal parts using a dampened very sharp knife. Repeat with the remaining ingredients. Serve the sushi cut-side up, with small bowls of soy sauce and wasabi.

MAKES 24

RIGHT: ROLLED SUSHI

SATAY WITH LONTONG

Lontong is an Indonesian recipe which constricts rice as it cooks so that the expanding grains form a mass which can be cut into squares. Traditionally, a banana leaf was used to make the container, but a boil-in-the-bag sachet is the ideal alternative. Lontong is always eaten cold and should be cooked the previous day or allowed to cool for at least 6 hours before serving.

350 g (12 oz) PORK FILLET, THINLY SLICED
PEANUT SAUCE, SEE BELOW, TO SERVE

Marinade
15 ml (1 tbsp) SOY SAUCE
1 CLOVE GARLIC, CRUSHED
pinch each GROUND CORIANDER AND CHILLI POWDER
15 ml (1 tbsp) OIL
2.5 ml (1/2 tsp) GROUND GINGER
5 ml (1 tsp) BROWN SUGAR

Lontong
125 g (4 oz) SACHET BOIL-IN-THE-BAG LONG GRAIN WHITE RICE
SALT

Make the lontong first by lowering the rice sachet into a saucepan of boiling salted water. Cover and simmer for 1¼ hours, checking the water level once or twice. Add more boiling water if required.

Remove the sachet of rice, which will be plumped-up like a cushion, and leave to cool. Chill overnight. Slit the bag open and cut lontong into small cubes.

To make the satay, mix the marinade ingredients together. Add the pork, cover, and leave to marinate for several hours in the refrigerator. Preheat the oven to 180°C (350°F/Gas mark 4).

Divide the pork equally between eight short bamboo skewers that have been soaked in cold water for 20-30 minutes. Place on a wire rack on a baking sheet and cook in the oven for 20 minutes, turning once, until the pork is cooked through. Serve with lontong and peanut sauce. Also serve some raw vegetables in a bowl containing a little rice vinegar and water, if desired.

SERVES 4

PEANUT SAUCE

75 ml (5 tbsp) OIL
125 g (4 oz) BLANCHED, UNSALTED PEANUTS
2 SHALLOTS, QUARTERED
1 CLOVE GARLIC
1 GREEN CHILLI, SEEDED
1 sliver (10 g/1/4 oz) TERASI (SHRIMP PASTE)
or 2.5 ml (1/4 tsp) ANCHOVY PASTE
10 ml (2 tsp) TAMARIND OR LIME JUICE
2.5 ml (1/2 tsp) BROWN SUGAR
400 ml (14 fl oz) WATER
25 g (1 oz) CREAMED COCONUT, CHOPPED
juice of 1/2 LEMON

Heat 60 ml (4 tbsp) oil in a pan and fry the peanuts gently for 3 minutes. Drain. Chop the shallots, garlic, chilli and terasi finely in a food processor. Heat the remaining oil in a large frying pan and fry the shallot mixture for 1 minute. Add the tamarind or lime juice and sugar and cook for 1 minute. Add the water and bring to the boil, stirring.

Chop cooked peanuts finely in a food processor and stir into the pan. Simmer until the sauce thickens, stirring occasionally. Stir the creamed coconut into the peanut sauce and add lemon juice to taste.   SERVES 4

RIGHT: SATAY WITH LONTONG AND PEANUT SAUCE

RISI E BISI

Risi e Bisi is a thick rice and pea soup and the recipe originates from Venice. Serve as a substantial starter or as a light lunch with some warm crusty Italian bread.

50 g (2oz) UNSALTED BUTTER

15 ml (1 tbsp) OIL

1 ONION, FINELY CHOPPED

3 SLICES STREAKY BACON, RINDED AND CHOPPED

450 g (1 lb) SHELLED FRESH OR FROZEN PEAS

250 g (9 oz) RISOTTO RICE

1.4 litres (2½ pints) HOT MEAT OR CHICKEN STOCK

50 g (2 oz) FRESHLY GRATED PARMESAN CHEESE

30 ml (2 tbsp) FRESHLY CHOPPED FLAT-LEAVED PARSLEY

Heat half the butter with the oil in a large saucepan and fry the onion and bacon until tender. If using fresh peas, add to the onions together with 30 ml (2 tbsp) stock and cook for 5 minutes. Add the rice and cook, stirring, for 2 minutes. Pour on the hot stock. Bring to the boil. Cover and simmer for 15-20 minutes. If using frozen peas, add them after 10 minutes.

Stir in the remaining butter, cheese and parsley. The mixture should resemble a very thick soup. Add a little extra hot stock before stirring in the butter, cheese and parsley, if the soup is too similar to a risotto.   SERVES 6

GUMBO

Gumbo is a Cajun dish for which there is no one definitive recipe. Some gumbos are thickened with okra, others with gumbo file, which is ground sassafras leaves, but they always commence with a roux.

25 g (1 oz) BUTTER

15 ml (1 tbsp) OIL

30 ml (2 tbsp) FLOUR

75 g (3 oz) BELLY PORK, CHOPPED INTO SMALL PIECES

1 LARGE ONION, SLICED

2 STICKS CELERY, CHOPPED

450 g (1 lb) FRESH OKRA, SLICED

397 g (14 oz) CAN PEELED TOMATOES

2 CLOVES GARLIC, CRUSHED

1 litre (1¾ pints) CHICKEN STOCK

175 g (6 oz) LONG GRAIN WHITE RICE

225 g (8 oz) PEELED COOKED PRAWNS

450 g (1 lb) COOKED CHICKEN, CHOPPED INTO SMALL PIECES

5 ml (1 tsp) TABASCO

Heat the butter and oil in a saucepan. Stir in the flour and cook over a low heat, stirring to make a rich brown roux (be careful not to let it burn).

In a large saucepan, fry the pork, until golden brown, add the onion and celery, and fry for 5 minutes. Then stir in the okra and fry for 3 more minutes. Add the tomatoes and their juice and the garlic, and simmer for 15 minutes.

Slowly pour the stock into the browned roux, stirring constantly. Bring to the boil, stirring, and simmer for 1 minute. Stir into the okra mixture. Cover and simmer for about 1 hour.

Meanwhile cook the rice as directed on page 14. Add the prawns and chicken to the gumbo 5 minutes before the end of cooking. Season with the Tabasco. Spoon into individual bowls and top with a scoop of hot cooked rice.   SERVES 6

TOP: RISI E BISI
BOTTOM: GUMBO

SALADS

Rice adapts well to cold salads, as it is simple to prepare in advance and reasonable in cost. Rice salads are perfect for serving large numbers of guests at barbecues, buffets or lunches. Moulded salads are unusual and particularly appropriate for special occasions.

CHINESE CHICKEN SALAD WITH PEANUT DRESSING

277 g (9.7 oz) can LONG GRAIN WHITE OR BROWN RICE
350 g (12 oz) COLD COOKED CHICKEN, SHREDDED
4 SPRING ONIONS, SLICED DIAGONALLY
125 g (4 oz) BUTTON MUSHROOMS, SLICED
50 g (2 oz) BEANSPROUTS, BLANCHED
1/4 CUCUMBER, CUT INTO THIN STRIPS

Peanut Dressing
30 ml (2 tbsp) WHOLENUT PEANUT BUTTER
1 SMALL CLOVE GARLIC, CRUSHED
10 ml (2 tsp) GRATED FRESH GINGER
15 ml (1 tbsp) each LIGHT SOY SAUCE, WINE VINEGAR AND SESAME OIL
30 ml (2 tbsp) each WATER AND FRESHLY CHOPPED CORIANDER

Cook the rice as directed on the can. Cool. Combine the rice with the remaining salad ingredients. Whisk the peanut dressing ingredients together until well blended, and pour over the salad ingredients and stir well. Chill for 1 hour to allow the flavours to blend.

SERVES 4

HOT CHICKEN RICE SALAD

700 g (1 1/2 lb) COOKED CHICKEN, IN BITE-SIZE PIECES
500 g (18 oz) COOKED EASY-COOK LONG GRAIN WHITE RICE
1 SMALL ONION, FINELY CHOPPED
1 WHOLE CANNED PIMENTO, CHOPPED
425 g (15 oz) CAN CREAM OF CHICKEN SOUP
425 g (15 oz) CAN CREAM OF CELERY SOUP
125 ml (4 fl oz) MAYONNAISE
4 STICKS CELERY, CHOPPED
75 g (3 oz) FLAKED ALMONDS
5 ml (1 tsp) GARLIC SALT
50 g (2 oz) GRATED CHEESE
50 g (2 oz) RICE KRISPIES, CRUSHED

Preheat the oven to 180°C (350°F/Gas mark 4). Mix all the ingredients together, except the Rice Krispies. Transfer to a large buttered casserole dish. Sprinkle with the Rice Krispies and bake in the oven for 30 minutes until golden.

SERVES 8

RIGHT: CHINESE CHICKEN SALAD WITH PEANUT DRESSING

CALIFORNIA SUNSHINE RICE MOULD

75 g (3 oz) EASY-COOK LONG GRAIN WHITE OR
BROWN RICE
1/2 x 425 g (15 oz) CAN CRUSHED PINEAPPLE
135 g (4.7 oz) PACKET LEMON JELLY
2 SMALL CARROTS, SCRAPED AND GRATED
50 g (2 oz) SEEDLESS RAISINS

To Garnish
2 ORANGES, PEELED AND SEGMENTED
50 g (2 oz) HALVED PECAN NUTS
LETTUCE

Cook the rice as directed on page 14. Drain the pineapple, reserving the juice. Make up the jelly as directed on the packet using the drained juice from the pineapple, plus water.

Pour half the jelly into a 1 litre ($1^3/_4$ pint) mould. Add the pineapple, carrots and raisins. Allow to set. Keep the remaining jelly so it is just on the point of setting. Mix the remaining jelly with the cooked rice and pour over the set jelly. Chill in the refrigerator until set. Unmould and fill the centre with the orange segments, pecan nuts and lettuce.   SERVES 6

TOSSED AVOCADO RICE SALAD

277 g (9.7 oz) CAN LONG GRAIN WHITE OR BROWN RICE
grated zest of 1 LEMON
25 g (1 oz) SUNFLOWER SEEDS, TOASTED
1 STICK CELERY, SLICED
220 g (7.7 oz) CAN RED KIDNEY BEANS, DRAINED
2 LARGE SPRING ONIONS, THINLY SLICED
1 LARGE RIPE AVOCADO
juice of 1/2 LEMON
30 ml (2 tbsp) VINAIGRETTE DRESSING

Cook the rice as directed on the can. Cool. Mix the rice and lemon zest together. Place sunflower seeds, celery, kidney beans and spring onions into a bowl. Peel, stone and roughly chop the avocado. Add to the vegetables with the lemon juice and vinaigrette dressing, and mix well. Arrange a circle of rice on two plates, then fill the centre with the avocado mixture. Serve immediately.   SERVES 2

MELON & PRAWN SALAD

500 g (18 oz) PACKET FROZEN PILAU RICE
1/2 SMALL MELON; GALIA, OGEN OR
CHARENTAIS
15 ml (1 tbsp) FRESHLY CHOPPED DILL
225 g (8 oz) FRESH PEELED PRAWNS
1/2 CRISP LETTUCE, WASHED AND TORN INTO
SMALL PIECES

Cook the rice according to the packet instructions. Allow the rice to cool. Remove the seeds from the melon and cut the flesh into cubes or balls. Stir the melon into the rice with the dill and prawns. Line a dish with lettuce and pile the rice mixture on top.   SERVES 4

TOP: CALIFORNIA SUNSHINE RICE MOULD
BOTTOM: TOSSED AVOCADO RICE SALAD

THREE-RICE PARTY SALAD

This multicoloured salad makes an attractive party dish. If desired, reheat the salad and serve warm for a buffet.

250 g (9 oz) WILD RICE

250 g (9 oz) LONG GRAIN BROWN RICE

250 g (9 oz) LONG GRAIN WHITE RICE

1.25 ml (¼ tsp) ENGLISH MUSTARD POWDER

juice of 1 LARGE LEMON

120 ml (8 tbsp) WALNUT OIL

3 SHALLOTS, FINELY CHOPPED

60 ml (4 tbsp) FRESHLY CHOPPED MIXED HERBS

Cook the three types of rice separately, as directed on page 14. When cooked, immediately spoon all the rices together into one large shallow dish to cool.

Whisk the mustard powder, lemon juice and walnut oil together. Stir into the rice with the shallots and herbs. Refrigerate for 2 hours to allow the flavours to blend. Serve cold. SERVES 18

CORONATION RICE SALAD

This salad is a vegetarian version of the classic Coronation Chicken. The blend of spiced mayonnaise and dressing is absorbed by the Quorn and rice imparting a variety of flavours to the final dish. You can substitute easy-cook long grain white rice for the basmati rice in this recipe.

350 g (12 oz) EASY-COOK BASMATI WHITE RICE

900 ml (1 ½ pints) WATER

4 CARDAMOM PODS, CRUSHED

200 ml (7 fl oz) MAYONNAISE

142 ml (¼ pint) CARTON SINGLE CREAM

10 ml (2 tsp) GARAM MASALA

432 g (15½ oz) CAN PINEAPPLE SLICES, WITH JUICE

250 g (9 oz) PACKET QUORN

1 RED PEPPER, SEEDED AND THINLY SLICED

1 GREEN PEPPER, SEEDED AND THINLY SLICED

125 g (4 oz) GREEN GRAPES, SEEDED AND HALVED

125 g (4 oz) BLACK GRAPES, SEEDED AND HALVED

1 STAR FRUIT, SLICED VERTICALLY

60 ml (4 tbsp) WALNUT OIL

15 ml (1 tbsp) WINE VINEGAR

Put rice, water and cardamom pods into a large saucepan. Cook the rice as directed on page 14. Drain and cool.

Meanwhile blend together the mayonnaise, cream and garam masala in a large bowl. Stir in 45 ml (3 tbsp) pineapple juice and the Quorn. Cut the pineapple slices into bite-sized pieces. Add the vegetables and fruit to the mayonnaise mixture. Mix together the oil and vinegar and stir into the cooled rice. Mix well and leave until cold. Stir the mayonnaise mixture into the rice. Pile on to a large serving plate.

SERVES 8, OR 10 FOR A BUFFET PARTY

TOP: THREE-RICE PARTY SALAD
BOTTOM: CORONATION RICE SALAD

CHIRA-SUSHI

30 ml (2 tbsp) OIL
1 LARGE CARROT, CUT INTO THIN STRIPS
1 ONION, CHOPPED
1 STICK CELERY, SLICED
50 g (2 oz) STICK BEANS, CUT INTO 2.5 CM (1 INCH) LENGTHS
50 g (2 oz) FROZEN PEAS
4 SHIITAKE MUSHROOMS, SLICED
1/2 x 198 g (7 oz) CAN SLICED BAMBOO SHOOTS, DRAINED
15 ml (1 tbsp) SOY SAUCE
5 ml (1 tsp) SUGAR
125 g (4 oz) COOKED PEELED PRAWNS
FINELY SLICED FRESH ROOT GINGER

Vinegared Rice

75 g (3 oz) SUGAR
50 ml (2 fl oz) RICE VINEGAR
2.5 ml (1/2 tsp) SALT
1 PIECE DRIED THIN LAVER, OPTIONAL
250 g (9 oz) GLUTINOUS WHITE RICE
400 ml (14 fl oz) WATER

Omelette

5 ml (1 tsp) OIL
1 (size 4) EGG, BEATEN
5 ml (1 tsp) WATER

To prepare the rice, dissolve the sugar in the rice vinegar over a low heat, add salt, then set aside. Put the dried laver, if used, into a saucepan with the water. When the laver has dissolved, add the rinsed rice. Cook the rice as directed on page 14. Tip the rice on to a large baking tray, and pour over the vinegar. Fan the rice with a rolled magazine or lid, while mixing the rice gently with a dampened wooden paddle or spoon. Continue until the rice is at room temperature.

For the omelette, heat the oil in a small omelette pan. Beat the egg with the water, then pour into the pan to coat the base evenly. Using a fork or spatula, lift the edges of the omelette, allowing the liquid to flow on to the pan. Continue until the omelette is nearly set. Transfer to a board and cut into thin strips.

Heat the oil in a frying pan and stir-fry the carrot, onion, celery and beans for 5 minutes. Add peas, mushrooms and bamboo shoots, and stir-fry for 2 minutes. Finally add the soy sauce and sugar. Heat through gently. Mix the vinegared rice with the cooked, cooled omelette, vegetables and prawns. Arrange in a serving dish and garnish with ginger.　SERVES 4

GADO-GADO

125 g (4 oz) SAVOY CABBAGE, SHREDDED
125 g (4 oz) STICK BEANS, CUT INTO SHORT LENGTHS
125 g (4 oz) CAULIFLOWER, CUT INTO FLORETS
125 g (4 oz) each CARROTS AND BEANSPROUTS
25 g (1 oz) GHEE OR CLARIFIED BUTTER
1 ONION, SLICED
1/4 CUCUMBER, SLICED
2 HARD-BOILED EGGS, QUARTERED
1 QUANTITY LONTONG AND PEANUT SAUCE, SEE PAGE 22

Steam the cabbage, beans, cauliflower, sliced carrots and beansprouts separately until tender. Heat the ghee in a frying pan and fry the onion until crisp. Reserve. Cool all the vegetables. Arrange the lontong in the centre of a large serving dish, and surround with the vegetables, cucumber and egg. Garnish the sauce with the fried onions and serve.　SERVES 4

TOP: GADO-GADO
BOTTOM: CHIRA-SUSHI

FRUITY RICE SALAD

175 g (6 oz) EASY-COOK LONG GRAIN WHITE RICE
125 ml (4 fl oz) VINAIGRETTE DRESSING
5 ml (1 tsp) GRATED ORANGE ZEST
10 ml (2 tsp) CLEAR HONEY
10 ml (2 tsp) ORANGE JUICE
2.5 ml ($1/2$ tsp) GROUND GINGER
2 ORANGES, SEGMENTED
40 g ($1^1/_2$ oz) SULTANAS
125 g (4 oz) GRAPES, HALVED AND SEEDED
$1/2$ PAPAYA, PEELED, SEEDED AND CHOPPED
1 MANGO, PEELED, STONED AND CHOPPED

Cook the rice as directed on page 14. Cool. Whisk together the vinaigrette dressing, orange zest, honey, orange juice, and ground ginger. Combine the cooled rice and all the fruit. Pour over the dressing and toss with a fork. Cover and refrigerate until required. Fluff up and serve.

SERVES 4

SPEEDY VEGETARIAN RICE SALAD

277 g (9.7 oz) CAN LONG GRAIN WHITE RICE
277 g (9.7 oz) CAN LONG GRAIN BROWN RICE
75 g (3 oz) FLAKED ALMONDS
390 g ($13^3/_4$ oz) CAN ARTICHOKE HEARTS, DRAINED AND HALVED
200 ml (7 fl oz) MAYONNAISE
5-10 ml (1-2 tsp) GARAM MASALA
SHREDDED ICEBERG OR WEBBS LETTUCE, TO SERVE

Cook the rices as directed on the cans. Cool. Toast the almonds until golden brown. Put the halved artichoke hearts and flaked almonds into a bowl. Add both the rices. Blend together the mayonnaise and garam masala and stir gently into the rice mixture. Serve on shredded lettuce.

SERVES 4

RIGHT: FRUITY RICE SALAD

SIDE DISHES

The following rice dishes are not substantial enough to serve as a complete meal, and are better suited alongside another dish. Many fish, seafood and chicken recipes are perfect for serving with rice, or choose one of your favourite ethnic dishes.

RICE PILAF

Pilafs owe their origin to Eastern Europe rather than India, home of the pilau. They often include dried fruit and nuts.

50 g (2 oz) BUTTER

1 LARGE ONION, SLICED

1 CLOVE GARLIC, FINELY CHOPPED

250 g (9 oz) EASY-COOK LONG GRAIN WHITE RICE

600 ml (1 pint) CHICKEN STOCK

2.5 ml ($\frac{1}{2}$ tsp) GROUND TURMERIC

125 g (4 oz) SULTANAS

1 LEMON

1 ORANGE

15 ml (1 tbsp) OIL

125 g (4 oz) CASHEW NUTS

125 g (4 oz) BUTTON MUSHROOMS

Heat the butter in a large saucepan and fry the onion and garlic for 2 minutes. Stir in the rice and cook for 2 minutes. Add the stock, turmeric and sultanas. Bring to the boil, stir, then lower the heat to simmer. Cover and cook for 15 minutes or until rice is tender and the liquid has been absorbed.

Cut thin strips of rind evenly from round the lemon and orange. Cut the lemon and orange into wedges. Blanch the lemon and orange strips in boiling water for a few minutes. Drain. Heat the oil and fry the nuts until golden brown. Drain on paper towels. Fry the mushrooms in the same oil until tender. Stir the nuts and mushrooms into the cooked rice. Serve garnished with the lemon and orange strips and wedges.

SERVES 4-6

FRIED RICE

250 g (9 oz) LONG GRAIN WHITE RICE

125 g (4 oz) SHELLED FRESH OR FROZEN PEAS

30 ml (2 tbsp) GROUNDNUT OIL

50 g (2 oz) CURED PORK OR PARMA HAM, CUT INTO THIN STRIPS

200 g (7 oz) BEANSPROUTS

2 (size 4) EGGS, BEATEN

CHOPPED SPRING ONIONS, TO GARNISH

Cook the rice as directed on page 14. Cool completely. Cook the fresh peas until tender. Drain. Heat the oil in a wok or large frying pan. Add the rice and stir-fry for 1 minute. Add the peas and pork or ham and continue to stir-fry over a high heat for 5 minutes. Stir in the beansprouts and the eggs and stir-fry until the egg is cooked. Transfer to a serving dish and garnish. SERVES 4-6

RIGHT: RICE PILAF

CHELO

This Persian dish is distinctive for its golden crusted rice grains and is best served with sauces and meat dishes. The crust is called Tah e dig and considered a delicacy. A variation in which other ingredients are cooked with the rice is called Polo.

large pinch SAFFRON THREADS, CRUSHED
250 g (9 oz) EASY-COOK LONG GRAIN WHITE RICE
125 g (4 oz) BUTTER

Soak the saffron in 15 ml (1 tbsp) hot water for 1 hour. Cook the rice as directed on page 14, but reduce the cooking time to 10 minutes when rice is barely tender. Drain through a sieve and rinse under warm water. Drain well, making holes in the rice with the handle of a wooden spoon to release steam and heat.

Melt half the butter in a deep saucepan. Add 30 ml (2 tbsp) water and stir until hot. Add the cooked rice, and stir until the rice is well-coated, then build the rice up into a cone shape. Melt remaining butter in a smaller saucepan, then pour the butter over the rice cone. Place a clean tea towel over the rice cone, and cover with a lid. Cook over a medium heat for 10 minutes, then reduce the heat to low and cook for 40 minutes. Do not remove the lid.

Spoon 45 ml (3 tbsp) of the cooked rice into a bowl and mix with the saffron liquid. Spoon the remaining rice into a serving dish - the rice at the bottom of the pan should have a crisp brown crust. If it does not, turn up the heat for a few minutes. Add the saffron rice to the serving dish and mix gently.   SERVES 4

SPICY BROWN RICE WITH VEGETABLES

30 ml (2 tbsp) OIL
2.5 ml (1/2 tsp) CHILLI POWDER
1.25 ml (1/4 tsp) GROUND TURMERIC
250 g (9 oz) LONG GRAIN BROWN RICE
625 ml (21 fl oz) FRESH VEGETABLE STOCK
1 LEEK, SLICED
75 g (3 oz) COURGETTES, THINLY SLICED
175 g (6 oz) CHESTNUT MUSHROOMS, SLICED
75 g (3 oz) VERY SMALL BROCCOLI FLORETS
50 g (2 oz) PINE KERNELS

Heat the oil in a saucepan and fry the spices and rice for 4 minutes. Pour on the vegetable stock, bring to the boil and stir. Lower the heat, cover and simmer for 20 minutes. Stir in the vegetables, cover and continue to simmer gently for 10 minutes. Stir in the pine kernels. Cover and simmer for another 5 minutes.

SERVES 4

TOP: SPICY BROWN RICE WITH VEGETABLES
BOTTOM: CHELO

HERBED LEMON RICE

grated zest and juice of 1 LEMON

250 g (9 oz) LONG GRAIN, BASMATI OR JASMINE WHITE RICE

60 ml (4 tbsp) FRESHLY CHOPPED MIXED HERBS

PARSLEY SPRIGS AND LEMON SLICES, TO GARNISH

Make up the lemon juice to the required amount of liquid with water. Pour into a saucepan. Add the lemon zest, rice and herbs. Cook by the absorption method as directed on pages 13 and 14. Garnish with parsley sprigs and lemon slices.

SERVES 4

SAFFRON RICE

2.5 ml (½ tsp) SAFFRON THREADS, CRUSHED

15 ml (1 tbsp) HOT WATER OR STOCK

250 g (9 oz) LONG GRAIN, BASMATI OR JASMINE WHITE RICE

Soak the saffron in 15 ml (1 tbsp) hot water or stock for 1 hour. Put the rice into a saucepan. Add the saffron liquid, including the saffron threads, and the required amount of water. Cook by the absorption method as directed on pages 13 and 14.

SERVES 4

CURRIED RICE

10 ml (2 tsp) OIL

1 ONION, FINELY CHOPPED

250 g (9 oz) LONG GRAIN, BASMATI OR JASMINE WHITE RICE

15 ml (1 tbsp) MILD CURRY POWDER OR HOT CURRY POWDER, SEE BELOW

Mild Curry Powder

15 ml (1 tbsp) each GREEN PEPPERCORNS, CARDAMOM SEEDS, CLOVES AND CUMIN SEEDS

5 ml (1 tsp) each GROUND CINNAMON AND GRATED NUTMEG

Hot Curry Powder

15 ml (1 tbsp) each GREEN PEPPERCORNS, CORIANDER SEEDS, GROUND TURMERIC

5-10 ml (1-2 tsp) DRIED CHILLI FLAKES

5 ml (1 tsp) each GROUND GALANGAL OR GROUND GINGER AND CUMIN SEEDS

Heat the oil in a saucepan and fry the onion for 2 minutes. Add the rice and curry powder and continue to cook, stirring, for 3 minutes. Add the required amount of water, and cook by the absorption method, as instructed on pages 13 and 14.

Grind the spices for powder in a small blender or spice grinder, or with a pestle and mortar. The blends can be altered to suit individual tastes. Store the remaining curry powder in separate airtight glass jars. Use within 1 month.

CLOCKWISE:
SAFFRON RICE, MILD CURRIED RICE,
HOT CURRIED RICE, HERBED LEMON RICE

DIRTY RICE

This Louisiana recipe is so-named because the chicken livers colour the rice. It features the 'Trinity', which is the combination of celery, onion and green pepper used in many Cajun dishes.

30 ml (2 tbsp) OIL
1 ONION, CHOPPED
2 STICKS CELERY, CHOPPED
1 SMALL GREEN PEPPER, SEEDED AND CHOPPED
225 g (8 oz) CHICKEN LIVERS, VERY FINELY CHOPPED
5 ml (1 tsp) CAYENNE PEPPER
250 g (9 oz) LONG GRAIN WHITE RICE
500 ml (18 fl oz) HOT HOME-MADE CHICKEN STOCK

Heat the oil in a large saucepan and fry the onion, celery and green pepper for 5 minutes. Add the chicken livers and stir well until browned. Stir in the cayenne pepper and the rice. Cook for 1 minute. Stir in the chicken stock. Bring to the boil. Cover and simmer for 12 minutes until the rice is tender and the liquid has been absorbed.

SERVES 4-6

RED BEANS 'N' RICE

1 HAM HOCK
450 g (1 lb) RED KIDNEY BEANS, SOAKED OVERNIGHT
2.5 litres (5 pints) WATER
30 ml (1 tbsp) OIL
1 LARGE ONION, CHOPPED
2 STICKS CELERY, THINLY SLICED
3 CLOVES GARLIC, CRUSHED
2 BAY LEAVES
250 g (9 oz) LONG GRAIN WHITE RICE

Simmer the ham hock in 700 ml (1¼ pints) water for 1 hour. Drain and reserve stock in a measuring jug. Make up to 500 ml (18 fl oz) with water if necessary. Rinse the beans, put in a large saucepan with 2 litres (4 pints) water, bring to the boil and boil for at least 10 minutes. Lower the heat and simmer for 1 hour until tender, adding more water as necessary. When cooked, drain and mash a few times to give a creamy texture.

Heat the oil in a saucepan and fry the onion, celery and garlic. Add the bay leaves and cook gently for 5 minutes. Add the rice and ham stock. Bring to the boil and stir. Lower heat, cover, and simmer for 12 minutes. Add the beans to the rice, cook together for a further 5 minutes. Remove the bay leaves and fluff up the rice before serving.

SERVES 4-6

TOP: DIRTY RICE
BOTTOM: RED BEANS 'N' RICE

Risottos

A classic Italian risotto demands undivided attention in cooking, because the skill is to add hot stock (which should be kept simmering) gradually during cooking. Time is well spent in producing the traditional risotto, but there are a few alternative methods given for those who require quick meals.

Milanese Risotto

5 ml (1 tsp) SAFFRON THREADS, CRUSHED
700 ml (1¼ pints) HOT CHICKEN STOCK
25 g (1 oz) BUTTER
30 ml (2 tbsp) OLIVE OIL
2 CLOVES GARLIC, CRUSHED
1 LARGE SPANISH ONION, CHOPPED
250 g (9 oz) RISOTTO RICE
300 ml (½ pint) DRY WHITE WINE
75 g (3 oz) FRESHLY GRATED PARMESAN CHEESE
GENEROUS KNOB OF BUTTER
FRESHLY GRATED PARMESAN CHEESE

Soak the saffron in the hot chicken stock for 1 hour. Heat the butter and the olive oil in a large saucepan. Add the garlic and onion, and fry until soft. Add the rice and stir over a low heat for 2 minutes.

Add 300 ml (½ pint) chicken stock and cook gently, stirring, until the liquid has been absorbed, then add another 300 ml (½ pint) of stock. Repeat as before, then add the white wine. When this has been absorbed, add the remaining stock and cook gently, stirring, until the rice is tender. Stir in the cheese. Add a knob of butter, stir, and serve with cheese.   SERVES 3-4

Mushroom Risotto

15 g (½ oz) DRIED MUSHROOMS
300 ml (½ pint) HOT WATER
45 ml (3 tbsp) OLIVE OIL
1 ONION, FINELY CHOPPED
2 CLOVES GARLIC, CHOPPED
250 g (9 oz) RISOTTO RICE
125 g (4 oz) BUTTON MUSHROOMS
125 g (4 oz) CHESTNUT MUSHROOMS, SLICED
600 ml (1 pint) HOT FRESH VEGETABLE STOCK
15 g (½ oz) UNSALTED BUTTER
50 g (2 oz) FRESHLY GRATED PARMESAN CHEESE
15 ml (1 tbsp) CHOPPED FLAT-LEAVED PARSLEY

Soak the dried mushrooms in the hot water for 15 minutes. Heat the oil in a large pan and fry the onion and garlic gently for 10 minutes. Add the rice and cook for 5 minutes. Strain the dried mushrooms, reserving the liquor. Add all the mushrooms to the pan and stir. Stir in half the vegetable stock. Cook gently, stirring, until all the liquid has been absorbed. Add the remaining vegetable stock and repeat. Add the mushroom liquor and repeat. Stir in the butter and cheese. Garnish with parsley.   SERVES 4

TOP: MILANESE RISOTTO   BOTTOM: MUSHROOM RISOTTO

CERVELAT & PEPPER RISOTTO

30 ml (2 tbsp) OIL

25 g (1 oz) BUTTER

1 ONION, CHOPPED

2 RED PEPPERS, SEEDED AND CHOPPED

250 g (9 oz) RISOTTO RICE

1 litre (1³/₄ pint) HOT CHICKEN STOCK

15 ml (1 tbsp) TOMATO PURÉE

45 ml (3 tbsp) FRESHLY CHOPPED PARSLEY

125 g (4 oz) CERVELAT SAUSAGE, CUT INTO STRIPS

432 g (15.2 oz) CAN BORLOTTI BEANS, DRAINED

Heat the oil and butter in a large saucepan and cook the onion and peppers for 2 minutes. Add the rice and cook for 2 minutes. Stir in 300 ml (½ pint) stock and simmer gently, stirring occasionally until the liquid has been absorbed. Add another 300 ml (½ pint) stock and repeat as before. Stir in the tomato purée, 30 ml (2 tbsp) parsley, the cervelat, beans and another 300 ml (½ pint) stock. Simmer gently, stirring occasionally, until the stock has been absorbed. Add the remaining stock and simmer until the rice is cooked and creamy. Serve sprinkled with the reserved parsley.   SERVES 4

MICROWAVE PEPPERONI RISOTTO

Risottos cook well in the microwave, and almost any recipe can be adapted to this cooking method.

15 ml (1 tbsp) OLIVE OIL

25 g (1 oz) BUTTER

1 ONION, CHOPPED

250 g (9 oz) RISOTTO RICE

700 ml (1¹/₄ pint) HOT BEEF STOCK

1.25 ml (¹/₄ tsp) TABASCO

200 g (7 oz) PEPPERONI SAUSAGE, SKINNED AND SLICED INTO THIN STRIPS

16 STUFFED GREEN OLIVES

225 g (8 oz) COOKED VEGETABLES, SUCH AS PEAS, CARROTS OR GREEN BEANS

Put oil, butter and onion in a 2.3 litre (4 pint) glass bowl. Cover and cook on full power for 3 minutes. Add the rice and stir well until thoroughly mixed. Cover and cook on full power for 2 minutes. Add 300 ml (½ pint) of the stock, and stir well. Cover and cook on full power for 5 minutes. Add another 300 ml (½ pint) of the stock. Cover again and cook on full power for 5 minutes. Stir in remaining ingredients and stock. Cover and cook on full power for 10 minutes or until rice is cooked and creamy. Stand for 5 minutes before serving.

SERVES 4

RIGHT: CERVELAT & PEPPER RISOTTO

BROWN RICE VEGETABLE RISOTTO

25 g (1 oz) BUTTER
15 ml (1 tbsp) OIL
1 ONION, CHOPPED
1 BULB FENNEL, CHOPPED
1 RED PEPPER, SEEDED AND CHOPPED
225 g (8 oz) CHESTNUT MUSHROOMS, QUARTERED
250 g (9 oz) LONG GRAIN BROWN RICE
625 ml (21 fl oz) VEGETABLE STOCK
50 g (2 oz) FRESHLY GRATED PARMESAN CHEESE
15 ml (1 tbsp) FRESHLY CHOPPED CORIANDER

Heat the butter and oil in a large saucepan. Fry the onion and fennel for 3 minutes. Add the pepper and mushrooms and continue to cook, stirring, for 2 minutes. Add the rice, stir well, and cook for 1 minute. Add the stock, and bring to the boil. Stir once and lower the heat to simmer. Cover and cook very gently for 35 minutes until the rice is cooked and the liquid has been absorbed. Take off the heat and stir in the cheese and coriander. SERVES 3-4

HADDOCK & MUSSEL RISOTTO

15 ml (1 tbsp) OLIVE OIL
25 g (1 oz) BUTTER
1 ONION, CHOPPED
5 ml (1 tsp) GROUND TURMERIC
1 GREEN PEPPER, SEEDED AND SLICED
1 YELLOW PEPPER, SEEDED AND SLICED
250 g (9 oz) RISOTTO RICE
1 litre (1³/₄ pints) HOT VEGETABLE STOCK
450 g (1 lb) SMOKED HADDOCK FILLET, SKINNED AND CUT INTO LARGE CUBES
30 ml (2 tbsp) FRESHLY CHOPPED PARSLEY
150 g (5 oz) COOKED SHELLED MUSSELS
3 TOMATOES, PEELED AND CHOPPED

Heat the oil and butter in a large saucepan. Cook the onion until soft, then stir in turmeric, green and yellow peppers and rice. Cook, stirring continuously, for 2 minutes. Stir in 300 ml (½ pint) of the stock and simmer gently, stirring occasionally, until the liquid has been absorbed. Add another 300 ml (½ pint) stock and repeat as before. Carefully stir in haddock and parsley and another 300 ml (½ pint) stock. Simmer gently, stirring occasionally, until stock has been absorbed. Add the remaining stock and simmer until the rice is cooked and creamy. Stir in the mussels and tomatoes about 3 minutes before the end of cooking. SERVES 4

TOP: BROWN RICE VEGETABLE RISOTTO
BOTTOM: HADDOCK & MUSSEL RISOTTO

CHICKEN LIVER RISOTTO

The wine in this classic recipe is boiled rapidly to give a wonderful flavour to the sliced chicken livers.

25 g (1 oz) BUTTER
30 ml (2 tbsp) OIL
1 ONION, CHOPPED
250 g (9 oz) RISOTTO RICE
4 TOMATOES, SKINNED AND CHOPPED
8 CHICKEN LIVERS, SLICED
300 ml (½ pint) WHITE WINE
700 ml (1¼ pint) HOT CHICKEN STOCK
50 g (2 oz) FRESHLY GRATED PARMESAN CHEESE

Heat the butter and oil in a large saucepan. Add the onion and cook for 1 minute. Add the rice and stir over a low heat for 2 minutes. Add the tomatoes and chicken livers and cook for 5 minutes. Pour in the wine and boil rapidly until the liquid has been absorbed. Add 300ml (½ pint) stock. Cook, stirring frequently, until the liquid has been absorbed. Repeat with another 300 ml (½ pint) stock. Then add the remaining stock and cook gently, stirring, until the rice is cooked and creamy. Stir in the cheese. SERVES 4

CHICKEN RISOTTO

2 CHICKEN PORTIONS
about 700 ml (1¼ pints) WATER
1 BAY LEAF
25 g (1 oz) UNSALTED BUTTER
15 ml (1 tbsp) OIL
1 ONION, FINELY CHOPPED
250 g (9 oz) LONG GRAIN WHITE RICE
10 ml (2 tsp) RICE SEASONING
50 g (2 oz) FRESHLY GRATED PARMESAN CHEESE
15 ml (1 tbsp) FINELY CHOPPED FLAT-LEAVED PARSLEY

Skin and bone the chicken portions, reserving the skin and bones. Cut the chicken into small pieces. Put the skin and bones into a saucepan with the water. Add the bay leaf. Bring to the boil. Cover and simmer for 30 minutes. Cool, then strain the chicken stock into a measuring jug. Make up to 600 ml (1 pint), if necessary, with water.

Heat the butter and oil in a large saucepan. Fry the onion and chicken for 3 minutes. Add the rice and rice seasoning and cook for 2 minutes. Add the chicken stock. Bring to the boil. Stir once and lower the heat to simmer. Cover and cook very gently for 12 minutes until the rice is tender and liquid has been absorbed. Take off the heat and stir in the cheese and parsley.

SERVES 4

LEFT: CHICKEN LIVER RISOTTO   RIGHT: CHICKEN RISOTTO

STIR FRIES

Stir-frying was originally created by the Chinese, but has become immensely popular all over the world. Using the stir-frying technique results in a dazzlingly fast meal. It is healthy too, as only a small amount of oil is used. Frozen rice, purchased from supermarkets, is convenient and ideal for stir-frying.

SWEET & SOUR VEGETABLE STIR FRY

250 g (9 oz) BASMATI WHITE OR BROWN RICE
30 ml (2 tbsp) SUNFLOWER OIL
4 CARROTS, CUT INTO FINE STRIPS
1 ONION, SLICED
225 g (8 oz) FRESH BABY SWEETCORN
2 STICKS CELERY, CHOPPED
350 g (12 oz) CHINESE LEAVES, SLICED

Sauce
125 ml (4 fl oz) PINEAPPLE JUICE
15 ml (1 tbsp) CORNFLOUR
30 ml (2 tbsp) BROWN SUGAR
60 ml (4 tbsp) WINE VINEGAR
30 ml (2 tbsp) TOMATO KETCHUP

Cook rice as directed on page 14. To make the sauce, blend together the pineapple juice, cornflour, brown sugar, vinegar and ketchup. Bring to the boil and stir until thickened. Remove from the heat, cover, and keep warm.

Heat the oil in a wok or large frying pan until very hot but not smoking. Add the carrots, onion, sweetcorn and celery and stir-fry for about 5 minutes until tender but crisp. Add the Chinese leaves and continue to stir-fry for about 2 minutes until tender. Transfer the stir fry to a bed of the hot cooked rice and pour over the sauce. SERVES 4

ORIENTAL SEAFOOD STIR FRY

30 ml (2 tbsp) OIL
1 LARGE CARROT, SLICED DIAGONALLY
75 g (3 oz) FRESH BABY SWEETCORN
50 g (2 oz) MANGETOUT
225 g (8 oz) SHARK OR SWORDFISH STEAK, SKINNED AND CUT INTO STRIPS
30 ml (2 tbsp) each SOY SAUCE AND CLEAR HONEY
5 ml (1 tsp) GROUND GINGER
4 SPRING ONIONS, CUT INTO THIN STRIPS
400 g (14 oz) PACKET FROZEN THREE-GRAIN RICE OR OTHER FROZEN RICE

Heat the oil in a wok or large frying pan until very hot but not smoking. Stir-fry the carrot, sweetcorn and mangetout for 2 minutes. Stir in the shark strips and cook for 2 minutes. Add the soy sauce, honey and ground ginger, and cook for about 3 minutes, stirring occasionally. Stir in the onions and rice and cook over a moderate heat for 5 minutes. SERVES 2

TOP: SWEET & SOUR VEGETABLE STIR FRY
BOTTOM: ORIENTAL SEAFOOD STIR FRY

CURRIED VEGETABLE STIR FRY

30 ml (2 tbsp) SUNFLOWER OIL

50 g (2 oz) CASHEW NUTS

25 g (1 oz) SUNFLOWER SEEDS

1/2 SMALL GREEN CABBAGE, SHREDDED

1/2 SMALL CAULIFLOWER, IN FLORETS

1 CLOVE GARLIC, CRUSHED

1 SMALL ONION, SLICED

2.5 ml (1/2 tsp) HOT CURRY POWDER, SEE PAGE 40

2.5 ml (1/2 tsp) GROUND TURMERIC

350 g (12 oz) FROZEN YELLOW RICE

75 ml (3 fl oz) HOT VEGETABLE STOCK

Heat half the oil in a wok or large frying pan and fry the nuts and seeds until golden brown. Remove from the pan and drain on paper towels. Heat the remaining oil. Put the cabbage, cauliflower, garlic and onion into the wok and stir-fry for about 5 minutes, until the vegetables are tender but still crisp. Mix in the curry powder and turmeric and fry for 2 minutes. Stir in the frozen rice and stir-fry for 5 minutes until thoroughly heated. Add the stock and cook a further 2 minutes. Add the nuts and sunflower seeds.   SERVES 2

SPICY LIVER STIR FRY

30 ml (2 tbsp) MILK

15 ml (1 tbsp) TOMATO PURÉE

5 ml (1 tsp) CHILLI SAUCE

225 g (8 oz) LAMB'S LIVER, CUT INTO THIN STRIPS

125 g (4 oz) EASY-COOK LONG GRAIN WHITE RICE

15 ml (1 tbsp) OIL

225 g (8 oz) CARROTS, CUT INTO THIN STRIPS

225 g (8 oz) RUNNER BEANS, TOPPED, TAILED AND
        SLICED

225 g (8 oz) BEANSPROUTS

125 ml (1/4 pint) CHICKEN STOCK

Mix the milk, tomato purée and chilli sauce in a bowl, stir in the liver, and leave for two hours to marinate. Cook the rice as directed on page 14. Heat the oil in a wok or frying pan until very hot but not smoking, and stir-fry the carrots for 2 minutes. Add the beans and beansprouts and stir-fry for a further 2 minutes. Add the liver, marinade and stock and cook for a further 4 minutes. Serve with the hot cooked rice.   SERVES 4

RIGHT: CURRIED VEGETABLE STIR FRY

TURKEY STIR FRY

Frozen rice and vegetables are excellent in stir fries, providing an almost instant meal. Do ensure that the turkey breast is thoroughly defrosted before cooking.

350 g (12 oz) FROZEN TURKEY BREAST, DEFROSTED AND THINLY SLICED

60 ml (4 tbsp) SUNFLOWER OIL

15 ml (1 tbsp) SESAME SEEDS

1 RED PEPPER, SEEDED AND SLICED

4 SPRING ONIONS, CHOPPED

200 g (7 oz) FROZEN BABY SWEETCORN

125 g (4 oz) FROZEN MANGETOUT

700 g (1½ lb) FROZEN RICE

Heat half the oil in a wok or large frying pan until very hot but not smoking, and fry the turkey for 3-4 minutes, stirring continuously. Remove from the pan and keep warm. Pour the remaining oil into the wok and stir-fry the sesame seeds, red pepper and spring onions for 2 minutes. Add the sweetcorn and mangetout, and stir-fry for a further 5 minutes. Return the turkey to the pan, add the frozen rice and stir-fry for 5 minutes until thoroughly heated.   SERVES 4

THAI-STYLE RICE STIR FRY

Long grain rice can be substituted for jasmine rice in this recipe.

250 g (9 oz) JASMINE WHITE RICE

450 ml (¾ pint) CHICKEN STOCK OR COCONUT MILK (SEE PAGE 68)

45 ml (3 tbsp) GROUNDNUT OIL

2 CLOVES GARLIC, CRUSHED

4 SPRING ONIONS, 2 CHOPPED AND 2 SLICED

¼ CUCUMBER, CUT INTO THIN STRIPS

450 g (1 lb) FRESH MINCED LEAN PORK OR BEEF MINCE

2.5 cm (1 inch) PIECE OF FRESH ROOT GINGER, PEELED AND GRATED

30 ml (2 tbsp) LIGHT SOY SAUCE

30 ml (2 tbsp) DRY SHERRY

5 ml (1 tsp) CHILLI OIL, OPTIONAL

5 ml (1 tsp) CORNFLOUR BLENDED WITH

150 ml (5 fl oz) STOCK OR WATER

Cook the rice as directed on page 14 using stock or coconut milk instead of water. Cool. Heat 30 ml (2 tbsp) oil in a wok or large frying pan until very hot but not smoking, and stir-fry the rice. Add 1 crushed garlic clove, the chopped spring onions and the cucumber. Stir-fry for about 4 minutes. Pile in a mound on a serving plate and keep warm.

Heat the remaining oil in the wok or frying pan. Stir in the meat with the remaining garlic, sliced spring onions and ginger. Stir-fry for about 5 minutes until well browned and cooked. Mix in the soy sauce, sherry and chilli oil, if using. Heat for 1 minute, then stir in the blended cornflour and stock or water and stir until thickened. Spoon on top of the rice.   SERVES 4

RIGHT: TURKEY STIR FRY

CHILLI BEEF STIR FRY

350 g (12 oz) RUMP STEAK, CUT INTO THIN STRIPS
30 ml (2 tbsp) GROUNDNUT OIL
250 g (9 oz) PATTY PAN SQUASH, SLICED HORIZONTALLY
200 g (7 oz) SUGAR SNAP PEAS, TOPPED AND TAILED
225 g (8 oz) CHESTNUT MUSHROOMS, SLICED
125 g (4 oz) BEANSPROUTS
277 g (9.7 oz) CAN LONG GRAIN WHITE OR BROWN RICE
juice of 1 ORANGE

Marinade

10 ml (2 tsp) SOY SAUCE
10 ml (2 tsp) RICE WINE OR SHERRY
5 ml (1 tsp) GROUNDNUT OIL
2.5 ml (½ tsp) CHILLI FLAKES
2.5 ml (½ tsp) GROUND FENUGREEK
grated zest of 1 ORANGE

Mix the marinade ingredients together in a large bowl. Stir in the sliced beef and marinate for 30 minutes. Heat the oil in a wok or large frying pan until very hot but not smoking. Drain the beef, reserving the marinade. Add the beef to the pan and stir-fry for 2 minutes. Add the vegetables and stir-fry for 5 minutes. Stir in the rice, orange juice and reserved marinade, and stir-fry for 3 minutes.   SERVES 4

MICROWAVE TUNA STIR FRY

Stir fry recipes are successful in the microwave. Almost any recipe can be adapted to this cooking method. Always start with the harder ingredients first.

125 g (4 oz) EASY-COOK LONG GRAIN WHITE RICE
250 ml (9 fl oz) BOILING WATER
15 ml (1 tbsp) OLIVE OIL
4 SPRING ONIONS, CUT INTO 2.5 CM (1 INCH) LENGTHS
198 g (7 oz) CAN BAMBOO SHOOTS, DRAINED AND SLICED
125 g (4 oz) OYSTER MUSHROOMS, STALKS TRIMMED
50 g (2 oz) BEANSPROUTS, RINSED
3 CHINESE LEAVES, SLICED
1 HEAD RED CHICORY, SLICED
400 g (14.1 oz) CAN TUNA CHUNKS IN BRINE, DRAINED
15 ml (1 tbsp) OYSTER SAUCE
1 LIME
15 ml (1 tbsp) FRESHLY CHOPPED TARRAGON

Put the rice and boiling water into a glass bowl. Cover and cook on full power for 6 minutes. Stand for 10 minutes. Heat the oil in a large glass bowl on full power for 1 minute. Add the spring onions and bamboo shoots. Stir well to coat in oil. Cover and cook on full power for 3 minutes. Stir in the mushrooms, beansprouts, Chinese leaves, red chicory, tuna, oyster sauce, and grated zest and juice from half the lime. Cover and cook on full power for 3 minutes. Stir in rice and chopped tarragon. Garnish with the remaining lime half, cut into wedges.   SERVES 4

TOP: MICROWAVE TUNA STIR FRY
BOTTOM: CHILLI BEEF STIR FRY

STUFFINGS

Rice is as suitable as breadcrumbs in making stuffings, and can help stretch expensive cuts of meat or fish. For a stuffing which is interesting in appearance and taste, and especially suitable for entertaining, try including a wild rice mixture.

GREEK STUFFED PEPPERS

6 GREEN PEPPERS
2 CLOVES GARLIC, FINELY CHOPPED
1 ONION, FINELY CHOPPED
15 ml (1 tbsp) OIL
450 g (1 lb) LEAN MINCED BEEF
125 g (4 oz) LONG GRAIN WHITE RICE
25 g (1 oz) PINE KERNELS
397 g (14 oz) CAN CHOPPED TOMATOES
30 ml (2 tbsp) TOMATO PURÉE
300 ml (1/2 pint) BEEF STOCK
30 ml (2 tbsp) CHOPPED FLAT-LEAF PARSLEY
30 ml (2 tbsp) CHOPPED MINT
150 ml (1/4 pint) TOMATO JUICE

Preheat the oven to 180°C (350°F/Gas mark 4). Slice the tops from the peppers and discard the seeds. Fry the garlic and onion in the oil until softened. Add the meat and cook until brown. Stir in the rice and pine kernels. Drain the tomatoes, reserving the juice. Add the drained tomatoes, tomato purée, stock and herbs. Cover and simmer for 10 minutes. Fill the peppers loosely with the mixture. Stand the peppers in a large shallow baking dish. Brush with oil. Mix together the tomato juices and pour around the peppers. Bake, uncovered, for 35-40 minutes.   SERVES 6

STUFFED TOMATOES

Long grain rice can be substituted for risotto rice in this recipe.

4 BEEFSTEAK TOMATOES
30 ml (2 tbsp) OIL
1 SMALL ONION, FINELY CHOPPED
1 CLOVE GARLIC, CRUSHED
125 g (4 oz) RISOTTO RICE
300 ml (1/2 pint) HOT VEGETABLE STOCK
30 ml (2 tbsp) FRESHLY CHOPPED OREGANO
50 g (2 oz) FETA OR GOAT'S CHEESE, CHOPPED
3 SUN-DRIED TOMATOES, FINELY CHOPPED

Preheat the oven to 180°C (350°F/Gas mark 4). Slice the tops off the tomatoes. Scoop out the pulp and seeds. Drain the tomatoes upside down. Chop the pulp. Heat the oil in a large frying pan and fry the onion and garlic for 2 minutes. Add the rice and stir for 3 minutes. Pour over half the stock and cook, stirring, until the liquid has been absorbed. Add the pulp and the remaining stock. Simmer gently to absorb the liquid. Stir in the remaining ingredients. Fill the tomatoes loosely. Bake, uncovered, for 15 minutes.

SERVES 4

RIGHT: GREEK STUFFED PEPPERS AND STUFFED TOMATOES

WHOLE SALMON WITH SPECIAL RICE STUFFING

Halve the stuffing ingredients for a 1.8 kg (4 lb) fish, and cook for about 45 minutes.

3.2 kg (7 lb) WHOLE SALMON
25 g (1 oz) BUTTER
1 small ONION, FINELY CHOPPED
125 g (4 oz) CELERY, FINELY CHOPPED
250 g (9 oz) LONG GRAIN WHITE RICE
LONG STRIP OF LEMON ZEST
juice of 1 LEMON
5 ml (1 tsp) FRESH CHOPPED THYME
5 ml (1 tsp) FRESH CHOPPED BASIL
550 ml (19 fl oz) WATER
2.5 ml (½ tsp) GARLIC SALT
3.75 ml (¾ tsp) GROUND BLACK PEPPER
OIL FOR BRUSHING

Wipe the fish inside and out and pat dry. Remove the head and tail. Melt the butter in a saucepan. Add the onion and celery and cook gently for 4 minutes, until the vegetables are soft. Add the rice and cook for a further minute. Add the lemon zest, lemon juice, water, herbs, and seasonings. Bring to the boil. Stir once. Cover and simmer for about 15 minutes, or until liquid has been absorbed. Remove the lemon zest. Preheat the oven to 180°C (375°F/Gas mark 5).

Line a large baking dish with oiled foil. Lightly pack the stuffing into the fish and place the fish on the foil. Fold over the foil and seal. Wrap any excess stuffing in foil. Cook the salmon in the oven for 1¼ - 1½ hours; add the foil parcel of stuffing for the last 10-15 minutes. Serve hot or cold.   SERVES 14

WHOLE-WHEAT PANCAKES WITH WILD RICE & SALMON FILLING

300 ml (½ pint) SKIMMED MILK
1 (size 4) EGG, BEATEN
5 ml (1 tsp) SUNFLOWER OIL
125 g (4 oz) WHOLE-WHEAT FLOUR
50 g (2 oz) PLAIN FLOUR
LARD FOR FRYING

Filling
75 g (3 oz) MIXED LONG GRAIN AND WILD RICE
225 g (8 oz) COOKED FRESH SALMON, OR SMOKED TROUT FILLET, FLAKED
15 g (½ oz) FRESH DILL, CHOPPED
1 SPRING ONION, FINELY SLICED
200 ml (7 fl oz) CRÈME FRAÎCHE
15 ml (1 tbsp) LEMON JUICE
SPRIG DILL, TO GARNISH

Cook the rice as directed on the packet. Make the pancake batter by whisking the milk, egg and oil together. Add the flours and whisk until smooth. Set aside for 30 minutes. Mix together the fish, dill, spring onion, 60 ml (4 tbsp) crème fraîche, lemon juice and cooked rice.

To make the pancakes, heat a knob of lard in a frying pan. Add about 30 ml (2 tbsp) of the batter. Cook until lightly browned underneath and just set on top. Brown on the other side. Make seven more.

Meanwhile heat the filling gently. Fold the pancakes in quarters and fill with the rice mixture. Serve garnished with the remaining crème fraîche and dill.

SERVES 8 AS A STARTER, 4 AS A MAIN COURSE

TOP: WHOLE SALMON WITH SPECIAL RICE STUFFING
BOTTOM: WHOLE-WHEAT PANCAKES WITH WILD RICE & SALMON FILLING

CAMPHOUSE TROUT WITH RICE STUFFING

4 TROUT, EACH WEIGHING ABOUT 300 G
(10 OZ), CLEANED AND GUTTED

OIL FOR BRUSHING

LIME SLICES, TO GARNISH

Stuffing

125 g (4 oz) LONG GRAIN BROWN RICE

50 g (2 oz) PINE KERNELS

125 g (4 oz) BUTTON MUSHROOMS, SLICED

5 ml (1 tsp) LEMON JUICE

PAPRIKA PEPPER

Preheat the oven to 180°C (350°F/Gas mark 4). Cook the rice as directed on page 14. Cool. Mix the rice with the stuffing ingredients, adding paprika to taste. Divide the stuffing between the trout (any remaining can be heated and served with the trout) placing it in the cavity of each fish.

Place the trout in a roasting tin, brush with oil, and cover with foil. Bake for about 20 minutes, until the flesh flakes easily. Garnish with the lime slices, and serve with steamed asparagus, if desired. SERVES 4

COULIBIAKA

This Russian dish originally used buckwheat in place of rice. The traditional coulibiakas were very much larger than today's versions and had to be carried to the table by more than one person due to their size.

50 g (2 oz) LONG GRAIN WHITE OR BROWN RICE

30 ml (2 tbsp) OIL

1 ONION, FINELY CHOPPED

1 LARGE CLOVE GARLIC, CRUSHED

grated zest of 1 LEMON

30 ml (2 tbsp) FRESHLY CHOPPED PARSLEY

15 ml (1 tbsp) FRESHLY CHOPPED DILL

450 g (1 lb) FRESH OR DEFROSTED SMOKED HADDOCK
FILLET, SKINNED AND CUBED

500 g (1 lb 2 oz) PACKET FROZEN OR CHILLED PUFF PASTRY

3 (size 4) EGGS, HARD-BOILED AND SLICED

BEATEN EGG OR MILK, TO GLAZE

Preheat the oven to 200°C (400°F/Gas mark 6). Cook the rice as directed on page 14. Heat the oil in a small frying pan and cook the onion and garlic until soft. Transfer to a basin and add the rice, lemon zest, herbs and smoked haddock. Mix together gently.

Roll the pastry out thinly into a large rectangle, then trim to 40 x 30.5 cm (16 x 12 inch). Carefully lift the pastry on to a baking sheet. Spoon half the fish mixture on to one-half of the pastry, leaving a narrow border around outside edges. Cover with sliced egg, then spoon the remaining fish mixture over the top.

Make cuts 2.5 cm (1 inch) apart on the other side of the pastry to within 4 cm (1½ inches) of the three edges. Brush the edges of the pastry with water, then fold the pastry over the filling. Seal the edges well. Mark pastry with diagonal lines, then decorate with leaves cut from trimmings. Brush with egg or milk, then bake for 30-35 minutes. SERVES 6

LEFT: COULIBIAKA
RIGHT: CAMPHOUSE TROUT WITH RICE STUFFING

POUSSINS WITH PISTACHIOS & WILD RICE

50 g (2 oz) MIXED BASMATI AND WILD RICE

50 g (2 oz) UNSALTED BUTTER

50 g (2 oz) LEEK, SLICED

25 g (1 oz) SHELLED PISTACHIOS

grated zest of 1 ORANGE

2 POUSSINS, EACH WEIGHING ABOUT 425 G (15 OZ)

Preheat the oven to 190°C (375°F/Gas mark 5). Cook the rice as directed on the packet. Melt 15 g ($^1/_2$ oz) butter and cook the leek until soft. Stir in the pistachios, orange zest and cooked rice, then mix well. Use some of the mixture to loosely stuff each bird. Place poussins in a roasting tin, dot each with the remaining butter, then roast for 50 minutes, basting occasionally. Reheat the remaining stuffing in a small saucepan or a microwave oven and serve with the birds, along with vegetables of your choice. SERVES 2

STUFFED PORK CHOPS WITH ORANGE RICE

This stuffing is also suitable for turkey escalopes or boneless chicken breasts.

8 PORK CHOPS, ON THE BONE

OIL, FOR BRUSHING

Stuffing

15 g ($^1/_2$ oz) BUTTER

2 SHALLOTS, FINELY CHOPPED

125 g (4 oz) LONG GRAIN BROWN RICE

325 ml (11 fl oz) VEGETABLE STOCK

1 SMALL ORANGE

50 g (2 oz) PITTED PRUNES, FINELY CHOPPED

50 g (2 oz) ROASTED HAZELNUTS, CHOPPED

1 (size 4) EGG, BEATEN

To make the stuffing, heat the butter in a saucepan and cook the shallots for 2 minutes. Add the rice and cook, stirring, for 1 minute. Pour in the stock. Bring to the boil. Stir once, then cover and simmer gently for 35 minutes until the rice is tender and the liquid has been absorbed. Cool. Preheat the oven to 190°C (375°F/Gas mark 5), or preheat the grill.

Meanwhile, grate the orange zest, remove the pith and chop the orange flesh into small pieces. Mix together the orange zest and flesh, the prunes, hazelnuts, cooled rice and the egg.

Trim the fat from each pork chop and use a sharp knife to slice the meat horizontally to make a pocket. Fill each cavity with the stuffing and secure with skewer or string. Brush the chops with oil and bake for 20 minutes or cook under the hot grill for 15 minutes, turning once during cooking. Remove the skewers or string before serving. SERVES 4-8

TOP: POUSSINS WITH PISTACHIO & WILD RICE
BOTTOM: STUFFED PORK CHOPS WITH ORANGE RICE

Main Dishes

Many acclaimed international dishes are accompanied by plain or lightly spiced rice, allowing the flavour of the main dish to be enhanced by the simplicity of the rice. Chicken Provençal, for example, is served with rice that has been flavoured with just oregano and lemon.

Thai Chicken with Jasmine Rice

4 BONELESS, SKINNED CHICKEN THIGHS
30 ml (2 tbsp) OIL
1 LARGE ONION, VERY FINELY CHOPPED
1 FRESH GREEN CHILLI, FINELY CHOPPED
30 ml (2 tbsp) each NAM PLA (FISH SAUCE) AND KETCHUP
juice of 1 LIME
1 STALK FRESH LEMON GRASS, SPLIT

Stuffing
225 g (8 oz) FRESH MINCED PORK
3 CLOVES GARLIC, CRUSHED
10 PEPPERCORNS, GROUND
grated zest of 1 LIME
30 ml (2 tbsp) FRESHLY CHOPPED CORIANDER

Rice Mixture
50 g (2 oz) COCONUT MILK POWDER
250 g (9 oz) JASMINE WHITE RICE

Mix all the ingredients for the stuffing together. Beat out the chicken thighs thinly between sheets of greaseproof paper. Divide the stuffing between the chicken thighs, then roll up. Secure with string. Heat the oil and brown the chicken for about 10 minutes, turning frequently. Lift out the chicken.

Fry the onion and chilli for about 3 minutes. Stir in the remaining ingredients. Replace the chicken, cover, and simmer for about 30 minutes, turning occasionally.

For the rice, whisk the coconut milk powder into 450 ml ($^3/_4$ pint) of water. Pour into a large saucepan. Add the rice. Bring to the boil, then stir once. Cover and simmer for 10 minutes until tender. Remove string from the chicken and lemon grass from the sauce. Slice and serve on a bed of the rice.   SERVES 4

Chicken Provençal

30 ml (2 tbsp) OIL
1 LARGE ONION, SLICED
4 CHICKEN BREASTS, SKINNED
30 ml (2 tbsp) each FLOUR AND TOMATO PURÉE
397 g (14 oz) CAN CHOPPED TOMATOES
125 ml (4 fl oz) DRY WHITE WINE
1 CLOVE GARLIC, CRUSHED
30 ml (2 tbsp) FRESHLY CHOPPED OREGANO
250 g (9 oz) EASY-COOK LONG GRAIN WHITE RICE
peeled zest of 1 LEMON

Preheat the oven to 180°C (350°F/Gas mark 4). Heat the oil in a casserole. Add onion and fry for 3 minutes. Coat the chicken in the flour, add to the pan. Cook until golden brown. Mix together the tomatoes, tomato purée, dry white wine, garlic and half of the oregano. Pour over the chicken. Cover and bake for 30 minutes. Cook the rice as directed on page 14. Stir the remaining oregano and lemon zest into the rice.   SERVES 4

RIGHT: THAI CHICKEN WITH JASMINE RICE

LAMB VINDALOO WITH SPICED RICE

2 LARGE CLOVES GARLIC, CRUSHED

15 ml (1 tbsp) GROUND GINGER

5 ml (1 tsp)each HOT CHILLI POWDER, GROUND CORIANDER,
CUMIN SEEDS AND GROUND CARDAMOM

2.5 ml (1/2 tsp) GROUND CLOVES

7.5 cm (3 inch) length CINNAMON STICK, LIGHTLY CRUSHED

150 ml (1/4 pint) WINE VINEGAR

1 kg (2 1/4 lb) LEAN LAMB, CUBED

60 ml (4 tbsp) GHEE OR CLARIFIED BUTTER

2 BAY LEAVES AND 12 PEPPERCORNS

Spiced Rice

30 ml (2 tbsp) OIL

50 g (2 oz) CASHEW NUTS

1 ONION, THINLY SLICED

1 CLOVE GARLIC, CRUSHED

350 g (12 oz) BASMATI WHITE RICE

5 ml (1 tsp) each GRATED FRESH ROOT GINGER AND
GARAM MASALA

large pinch of CAYENNE PEPPER

about 900 ml (1 1/2 pints) HOT VEGETABLE STOCK

15 ml (1 tbsp) FRESHLY CHOPPED CORIANDER

Put the garlic and spices into a bowl with the vinegar. Stir in the meat, cover and leave to marinate in refrigerator for about 24 hours.

Heat the ghee in a saucepan, toss in the meat, spices and vinegar with the bay leaves and peppercorns. Cover with a tight-fitting lid and simmer gently over a low heat for about 1 hour. Remove the lid and simmer for a further 15 minutes to thicken the juices.

For the rice, heat the oil in a saucepan and brown the cashew nuts. Remove with a slotted spoon and reserve. Stir the onion into the pan and cook until just beginning to brown. Stir in the garlic, rice and spices, and continue cooking for 3 minutes, stirring. Stir in the hot stock. Cover and simmer for 10 minutes, until the rice is tender and the liquid absorbed. Stir in the nuts and sprinkle with coriander. Serve with the lamb.

SERVES 6

CHICKEN KORMA WITH BASMATI RICE

45 ml (3 tbsp) GHEE OR CLARIFIED BUTTER

1 LARGE ONION, FINELY SLICED

2.5 ml (1/2 tsp) MILD CHILLI POWDER

2.5 ml (1/2 tsp) GROUND TURMERIC

10 ml (2 tsp) GARAM MASALA

200 ml (7 fl oz) WATER

2.5 cm (1 inch) piece FRESH GINGER, SLICED

1 CLOVE GARLIC, SLICED

4 CHICKEN PORTIONS, HALVED AND SKINNED

142 ml (1/4 pint) NATURAL YOGURT

2.5 ml (1/2 tsp) CUMIN SEEDS

2.5 ml (1/2 tsp) CLOVES

1.25 ml (1/4 tsp) GROUND BLACK PEPPER

250 g (9 oz) BASMATI WHITE RICE

Heat the ghee in a saucepan and fry the onion until crisp. Reserve. Mix the chilli, turmeric and garam masala with the water and pour into the pan. Bring to the boil. Simmer for 3 minutes. Add ginger, garlic and chicken. Stir well, cover, and simmer for 20 minutes.

Turn the chicken over in the pan, then simmer, uncovered, for a further 30 minutes until the liquid has almost evaporated. Crush the crisp onion. Add the crushed onion, yogurt and remaining spices. Simmer until the sauce is very thick. Cook rice as directed on page 14. Serve the chicken with the rice.   SERVES 4

TOP: CHICKEN KORMA   BOTTOM: LAMB VINDALOO

FISH CREOLE

250 g (9 oz) LONG GRAIN WHITE RICE

15 ml (1 tbsp) OIL

1 CLOVE GARLIC, CRUSHED

1 LEEK, SLICED

1 GREEN PEPPER, SEEDED AND SLICED

2.5 cm (1 inch) piece ROOT GINGER, PEELED AND FINELY CHOPPED

10 ml (2 tsp) GROUND CORIANDER

5 ml (1 tsp) GROUND CUMIN

5 ml (1 tsp) PAPRIKA PEPPER

15 ml (1 tbsp) FLOUR

150 ml (5 fl oz) FISH OR VEGETABLE STOCK

397 g (14 oz) CAN CHOPPED TOMATOES

1 BAY LEAF

450-700 g (1-1½ lb) HUSS, POLLACK OR COD FILLETS, SKINNED AND CUBED

8 STUFFED GREEN OLIVES, SLICED

15ml (1 tbsp) SUNFLOWER SEEDS

Cook the rice as directed on page 14. Meanwhile, heat the oil in a large saucepan and cook the garlic, leek, green pepper and ginger for 5 minutes. Stir in the ground spices and flour, and cook for about 1 minute. Gradually stir in the stock and tomatoes. Bring to the boil, stirring until the sauce thickens. Add the bay leaf. Simmer, uncovered, for about 10 minutes. Add the fish and simmer for a further 7-10 minutes. Discard the bay leaf. Stir the olives and sunflower seeds into the cooked rice and serve with the fish.   SERVES 4

BOBOTIE

Bobotie is a South African dish consisting of an unusual curried meat mixture topped by a savoury custard.

700 g (1½ lb) COARSE-CUT MINCED BEEF OR LAMB

1 ONION, CHOPPED

15 ml (1 tbsp) MILD CURRY POWDER, SEE PAGE 40

5 ml (1 tsp) GROUND TURMERIC

grated zest and juice of ½ LEMON

397 g (14 oz) CAN CHOPPED TOMATOES

2 SLICES WHITE BREAD, CRUSTS REMOVED

325 ml (11 fl oz) SEMI-SKIMMED MILK

25 g (1 oz) CHOPPED ALMONDS

50 g (2 oz) SEEDLESS RAISINS

15 ml (1 tbsp) MANGO CHUTNEY, CHOPPED

2 (size 4) EGGS

1 QUANTITY SAFFRON RICE, SEE PAGE 40

Preheat the oven to 180°C (350°F/Gas mark 4). Put the meat into a large saucepan. Stir gently to brown. Stir in the onion and cook for 5 minutes. Stir in the curry powder, turmeric, lemon zest and juice, and tomatoes, and simmer gently for 15 minutes.

Meanwhile, soak the bread in 30 ml (2 tbsp) of the milk. Stir the almonds, raisins and chutney into the meat. Squeeze the bread and tear into pieces. Add the bread to the meat and stir well. Transfer to a shallow 22.5 x 17.5 cm (9 x 7 inch) ovenproof casserole and cook in the oven for 30 minutes. Beat the remaining milk and the eggs together. Pour over the meat and return to the oven for a further 30 minutes or until custard has set. Serve with the rice.   SERVES 4-6

RIGHT: FISH CREOLE

BEEF TERIYAKI

575 g (1¼ lb) RUMP STEAK, CUT INTO THIN STRIPS
250 g (9 oz) GLUTINOUS WHITE RICE

Marinade
75 ml (3 fl oz) SOY SAUCE
30 ml (2 tbsp) SAKE OR SWEET SHERRY
1 ONION, SLICED
25 g (1 oz) FRESH ROOT GINGER, PEELED AND SLICED
15 ml (1 tbsp) LEMON JUICE
10 ml (2 tsp) SUGAR

Mix the marinade ingredients in a large shallow dish. Add the meat and leave to marinate for 1 hour, turning the meat over once or twice. Cook the rice as directed on page 14. Meanwhile, preheat the grill.

Remove the meat from the marinade and grill for 3-5 minutes, turning the meat once or twice and basting with the strained marinade. Spoon the hot rice into four oiled moulds or cups and quickly invert onto four plates. Arrange the meat beside the rice and pour over the warm basting juices from the grill pan.   SERVES 4

GOULASH OVER RICE

30 ml (2 tbsp) OIL
575 g (1¼ lb) LEAN PORK, TRIMMED AND CUBED
2 LARGE ONIONS, SLICED
900 ml (1½ pint) BEEF STOCK
45 ml (3 tbsp) TOMATO PURÉE
15-20 ml (3-4 tsp) PAPRIKA PEPPER
10 ml (2 tsp) SUGAR
15 ml (1 tbsp) PLAIN FLOUR
250 g (9 oz) LONG GRAIN WHITE OR BROWN RICE
60 ml (4 tbsp) SOURED CREAM

Heat the oil in a large saucepan and fry the pork and onion until sealed on all sides. Add the stock and simmer for 10 minutes. Remove a little stock from the pan and blend with the tomato purée, paprika, sugar and flour until smooth. Stir into the pan. Bring to the boil, stirring. Cover and simmer for 1½ hours or until the meat is tender. Cook the rice as directed on page 14. Just before serving, stir the soured cream into the meat and serve with the rice.   SERVES 4

CHILLI CON CARNE

450 g (1 lb) COARSE-CUT MINCED BEEF
1 LARGE ONION, CHOPPED
2 CLOVES GARLIC, CRUSHED
1 LARGE GREEN PEPPER, SEEDED AND CHOPPED
15 ml (1 tbsp) TOMATO PURÉE
432 g (15.25 oz) CAN RED KIDNEY BEANS
397 g (14 oz) CAN CHOPPED TOMATOES
5-10 ml (1-2 tsp) HOT CHILLI POWDER
250 g (9 oz) LONG GRAIN WHITE OR BROWN RICE

Put the meat into a large saucepan. Heat gently to brown, stirring frequently. Stir in the onion, garlic and green pepper and cook for 5 minutes, stirring. Stir in the tomato purée, kidney beans with the liquid, tomatoes with their juice and chilli powder to taste. Bring slowly to the boil. Cover and simmer for 45 minutes. Meanwhile cook the rice as directed on page 14. Serve the chilli con carne on the rice.   SERVES 4

RIGHT: BEEF TERIYAKI

ONE-POT MEALS

Most rice-growing countries have paid homage to their grain by devising a national dish. Generally cooked in one pot, the rice is mixed with other local ingredients. For example, in Cajun country in the USA, crawfish and sausage are mixed with rice to make Jambalaya, and, in Spain, seafood is mixed with rice to create Paella.

LAMB & TOMATO PILAF

A traditional dish from Eastern Europe in which all the ingredients are cooked together so the flavours will blend.

30 ml (2 tbsp) OIL
1 LARGE ONION, CHOPPED
350 g (12 oz) LEAN LAMB, CUT INTO SMALL CUBES
1 CLOVE GARLIC, CRUSHED
700 g (1½ lb) TOMATOES, SKINNED AND QUARTERED
2-3 BAY LEAVES
350 g (12 oz) EASY-COOK LONG GRAIN BROWN RICE

Heat the oil in a large saucepan and cook the onion and lamb over a gentle heat for 10 minutes. Stir in the garlic, cook for 15 seconds, then add the tomatoes and bay leaves. Cook for a further 10 minutes. Add the rice, cover with a tight-fitting lid, and cook over a gentle heat for 20 minutes. Discard the bay leaves. If desired, garnish with coriander and lime. SERVES 4

VEGETABLE PILAU

Although a pilau is similar to a pilaf, it is more highly spiced due to its Indian origins.

30 ml (2 tbsp) OIL
1 LARGE LEEK, SLICED
½ RED PEPPER, SEEDED AND DICED
4 STICKS CELERY, CHOPPED
2.5 ml (½ tsp) GROUND CARDAMOM
5 ml (1 tsp) PAPRIKA PEPPER
2.5 ml (½ tsp) GROUND CINNAMON
125 g (4 oz) BASMATI BROWN RICE
about 300 ml (½ pint) VEGETABLE STOCK
2 SMALL HEADS BROCCOLI, DIVIDED INTO FLORETS
1 SMALL CAULIFLOWER, DIVIDED INTO FAIRLY SMALL FLORETS

Heat the oil in a large frying pan and cook the leek, red pepper and celery for 2 minutes. Stir in the spices and rice, then gradually stir in the stock. Bring to the boil, add the broccoli and cauliflower, cover, then simmer gently for 25 minutes, stirring occasionally, until the rice is tender and the liquid has been absorbed. SERVES 2

RIGHT: LAMB & TOMATO PILAF

CHICKEN BIRYANI

The Biryani originated in the north of India, and was served during festivals. The meat is steamed in a yogurt-based marinade. You can substitute easy-cook long grain white rice for basmati rice in this recipe.

575 g (1¼ lb) CHICKEN BREAST FILLET, CUBED
30 ml (2 tbsp) GHEE OR CLARIFIED BUTTER
2 ONIONS, SLICED
250 g (9 oz) EASY-COOK BASMATI WHITE RICE
3 BAY LEAVES

Marinade
284 ml (10 fl oz) NATURAL YOGURT
15 ml (1 tbsp) GRATED FRESH GINGER
2 LARGE SPANISH ONIONS, GRATED
3 CLOVES GARLIC, CRUSHED
20-25 ml (4-5 tsp) HOT CURRY POWDER, SEE PAGE 40

To Garnish
2 HARD-BOILED EGGS, EACH CUT INTO 6
FRESHLY CHOPPED CORIANDER

Preheat oven to 190° C (375° F/Gas mark 5). Mix the ingredients for the marinade together. Stir in the chicken, cover, and leave in the refrigerator to marinate for at least 4 hours. Heat the ghee or clarified butter, then cook the onions until golden. Lift out the onion and reserve a little for a garnish. Turn the chicken with the marinade into a saucepan with the cooked onion.

Bring to the boil and cook, uncovered, over a low to medium heat for 15 minutes. Partly cook the rice in boiling water for 7 minutes. Drain. Place half the rice in a 2 litre (3 pint) casserole. Spoon the chicken and yogurt mixture over, then cover with the remaining rice. Gently press the rice into the liquid. Place the bay leaves on top. Cover with a tight-fitting lid and cook in the oven for 25 minutes until the rice is tender. Spoon on to a warm serving plate. Garnish with the reserved onion, egg and chopped coriander. SERVES 4

NASI GORENG

Nasi Goreng means fried rice and it can be served either as a meal in itself or alongside a selection of other Indonesian dishes. You can substitute long grain rice for jasmine rice in this recipe.

250 g (9 oz) JASMINE WHITE RICE
15 g (½ oz) BUTTER
2 (size 4) EGGS
10 ml (2 tsp) WATER
30 ml (2 tbsp) GROUNDNUT OIL
4 SHALLOTS, SLICED
1-2 FRESH GREEN CHILLIES, SEEDED AND
SLICED
225 g (8 oz) COOKED HAM, CUT INTO SMALL CUBES
125 g (4 oz) COOKED PEELED PRAWNS
125 g (4 oz) COOKED VEGETABLES, SUCH AS PEAS,
CARROTS, CABBAGE
5 ml (1 tsp) SOY SAUCE

Cook the rice as directed on page 14, but do not allow it to become too soft. Cool and set aside for 2 hours.

Heat the butter in an omelette pan. Beat the eggs with the water, then pour into the pan. Using a spatula, lift the edges, allowing liquid to flow on to the pan. Continue until nearly set. Cut into strips.

Heat the oil in a wok or large frying pan. Add the shallots and chillies and stir-fry for 1 minute. Add the ham, prawns and vegetables and stir-fry for 3 minutes. Add the cooked rice and stir-fry until it is thoroughly heated. Stir in the soy sauce. Transfer to a serving dish and arrange omelette strips on top. SERVES 3-4

RIGHT: CHICKEN BIRYANI

Jambalaya

Jambalaya is an infinitely adaptable dish traditionally made from leftovers and what was on hand. Cajun in origin, Jambalaya was a meal for the poor rural folk rather than their wealthier town cousins, the Creoles. This recipe uses chicken instead of crawfish.

30 ml (2 tbsp) OIL

4 CHICKEN JOINTS, BONED AND CUT INTO CHUNKS

225 g (8 oz) CHORIZO SAUSAGE, CUT INTO CHUNKS

1 LARGE ONION, SLICED

3 STICKS CELERY, SLICED

1 CLOVE GARLIC, CRUSHED

1 GREEN PEPPER, SEEDED AND SLICED

1 RED PEPPER, SEEDED AND SLICED

625 ml (21 fl oz) CHICKEN STOCK

250 g (9 oz) LONG GRAIN WHITE RICE

2.5 ml (½ tsp) CAYENNE PEPPER

2 BEEFSTEAK TOMATOES, SKINNED AND CHOPPED

Heat the oil in a large saucepan and brown the chicken. Add the sausage and cook with the chicken for a few minutes. Remove the chicken and sausage from the pan and keep warm.

Fry the onion, celery, garlic and peppers until tender. Return the chicken and sausage to the pan. Add the stock. Simmer for 15 minutes. Add the rice, tomatoes and cayenne pepper, bring back to the boil, and stir once. Lower the heat to simmer, cover, and cook for 15 minutes, until the rice is tender and the liquid has been absorbed.   SERVES 4

Kedgeree

During the days of the British Raj in India, it is believed that Kedgeree was adapted from Kichiri, an indigenous dish of rice and lentils. To speed up preparation, cook the rice the night before for a quick and easy breakfast.

25 g (1 oz) BUTTER

350 g (12 oz) SMOKED HADDOCK, COD OR WHITING FILLET, SKINNED AND CUBED

350 g (12 oz) COOKED LONG GRAIN WHITE RICE OR BASMATI WHITE RICE

15 ml (1 tbsp) FRESHLY CHOPPED PARSLEY

1 HARD-BOILED EGG, CHOPPED

pinch of GRATED NUTMEG

grated zest and juice of ½ LEMON

Melt the butter in a large saucepan, add the fish and cook gently for about 5 minutes, stirring occasionally. Stir in the cooked rice and cook for a further 4-5 minutes. Add the parsley, chopped egg, nutmeg and lemon juice. Cook, stirring, for a further 2 minutes, until piping hot. Garnish with the lemon zest and serve immediately.   SERVES 4

RIGHT: JAMBALAYA

PAELLA

Paella originated in Spain and is the name of the oval, two handled, metal pan in which this dish is cooked. Although recipes may vary, it is traditional to mix meat and fish in the ingredients.

large pinch of SAFFRON THREADS, CRUSHED
150 ml (5 fl oz) HOT WATER
30 ml (2 tbsp) OIL
50 g (2 oz) BUTTER
450 g (1 lb) CHICKEN BREAST FILLET, CUBED
1 LARGE ONION, CHOPPED
2 LARGE CLOVES GARLIC, CRUSHED
1 RED PEPPER, SEEDED AND CHOPPED
1 GREEN PEPPER, SEEDED AND CHOPPED
500 g (1 lb 2 oz) RISOTTO RICE
450 ml (^{3}/$_4$ pint) WHITE WINE
30 ml (2 tbsp) FRESHLY CHOPPED PARSLEY
2 LARGE BAY LEAVES
900 ml (1^1/$_2$ pints) HOT FISH STOCK
575 g (1^1/$_4$ lb) MIXED SHELLFISH, SUCH AS SCALLOPS, SQUID, COOKED PEELED PRAWNS AND COOKED MUSSELS

Soak the saffron in the hot water for 1 hour. Heat the oil and butter in a paella pan or 51 cm (20 inch) large frying pan. Cook the chicken for 5 minutes until brown, remove and keep warm. Cook the onion and garlic in the remaining fat until tender. Add the peppers and rice and cook for 2 minutes, stirring continuously. Stir in the saffron liquid, wine, parsley and bay leaves.

Simmer gently, stirring occasionally, until the liquid has been absorbed. Return the chicken to the pan with about 300 ml (^{1}/$_2$ pint) stock and cook as before. Stir in 300 ml (^{1}/$_2$ pint) stock, stirring occasionally. Stir in the remaining ingredients and another 300 ml (^{1}/$_2$ pint) stock and simmer gently until liquid has been absorbed and the rice is cooked and creamy.　SERVES 8

ARROZ CON POLLO

Rice with chicken is thought to owe its birth to either Portugal or Spain. Simpler than a paella, it nevertheless provides a substantial all-in-one complete meal.

4 CHICKEN PORTIONS
15 ml (1 tbsp) OLIVE OIL
20 ml (4 tsp) PAPRIKA PEPPER
5ml (1 tsp) SALT
125 ml (4 fl oz) WATER
300 ml (^{1}/$_2$ pint) CHICKEN STOCK
250 g (9 oz) EASY-COOK LONG GRAIN WHITE RICE
1 ONION, CHOPPED
1 GREEN PEPPER, SEEDED AND CHOPPED
1 GREEN CHILLI, SEEDED AND CHOPPED
397 g (14 oz) CAN CHOPPED TOMATOES

Preheat the oven to 220°C (425°F/Gas mark 7). Brush the chicken skin with oil and rub in the paprika pepper and salt. Pour the water into a large casserole. Put the chicken, skin-side up, in the casserole. Cook in the oven, uncovered, for 20 minutes. Remove the chicken from the casserole and keep warm. Lower the temperature to 190°C (375°F/Gas mark 5).

Pour the stock into the casserole, add the rice, onion, green pepper, chilli and canned tomatoes. Stir well. Arrange the chicken on top of the rice mixture. Cover tightly and cook for 45 minutes until the rice is tender and the liquid has been absorbed.　SERVES 4

TOP: ARROZ CON POLLO　BOTTOM: PAELLA

CHICKEN SIMMERED WITH RICE & LENTILS

Long grain brown rice can be substituted for basmati rice in this recipe.

15 ml (1 tbsp) OIL
7.5 cm (3 inch) length CINNAMON
3.75 ml (³/₄ tsp) CUMIN SEEDS
6 CLOVES
45 ml (3 tbsp) GHEE OR CLARIFIED BUTTER
1 ONION, SLICED
350 g (12 oz) CHICKEN BREAST FILLET, CUBED
350 g (12 oz) BASMATI BROWN RICE
1 litre (1³/₄ pints) HOT CHICKEN STOCK
125 g (4 oz) RED LENTILS
5 ml (1 tsp) GROUND CARDAMOM
125 g (4 oz) RAISINS
125 g (4 oz) ALMONDS, TOASTED
30 ml (2 tbsp) FRESHLY CHOPPED CORIANDER

Heat the oil in a large saucepan and cook the whole spices for 2 minutes over a low heat. Add the ghee or butter and the onion, then cook until the onion is golden. Stir in the chicken and cook for about 3 minutes. Stir in the rice and cook for 5 minutes.

Increase the heat and stir in the stock, lentils and cardamom. Bring to the boil, cover, and simmer gently for 20 minutes. Stir in the raisins and almonds, cover again, and cook for a further 5 minutes, or until the liquid has been absorbed and the rice is tender. Stir in the coriander.   SERVES 4

RICE À LA VALENCIA

Spain claimed the Philippines in 1521 and this dish, although inherently Spanish, is enhanced with a touch of the exotic in the form of coconut milk. Rice à la Valencia is served on large platters during Filipino festivals.

125 g (4 oz) BUTTER
6 CHICKEN JOINTS, SKINNED
225 g (8 oz) PORK, CUBED
1 ONION, SLICED
2 CLOVES GARLIC, CRUSHED
3 LARGE TOMATOES, SKINNED AND CHOPPED
50 g (2 oz) GARLIC SAUSAGE, SLICED
50 g (2 oz) COCONUT MILK POWDER
500 ml (18 fl oz) WARM WATER
350 g (12 oz) LONG GRAIN WHITE RICE
125 g (4 oz) FROZEN PEAS
30 ml (2 tbsp) GREEN OLIVES, STONED AND SLICED
2 HARD-BOILED EGGS, QUARTERED
1 PIMENTO, CUT INTO STRIPS

Heat half the butter in a large pan and fry chicken until brown, for about 10 minutes. Remove from the pan and keep warm. Brown the pork in the butter. Remove from the pan and keep warm. Add remaining butter to the pan and fry the onion, garlic, tomatoes and garlic sausage for 5 minutes. Return the chicken and pork to the pan. Cover and simmer for 15 minutes.

Whisk the coconut milk powder into warm water. Add the rice to the pan and stir in the coconut milk. Bring to the boil. Cover and simmer very gently for 10 minutes. Stir in the peas and olives and cook for a further 5 minutes or until rice is tender and liquid has been absorbed. Garnish with the hard-boiled eggs and pimento.   SERVES 6

RIGHT: CHICKEN SIMMERED WITH RICE & LENTILS

PUDDINGS & DESSERTS

Virtually every country has its own version of rice pudding, from plainly prepared recipes to elaborate concoctions. The basic ingredients are rice, milk and sugar, but often fruit is added. Also included in this chapter are more unusual rice desserts and treats, such as Calas Tous Chauds, which are rice fritters served with a sauce.

TRADITIONAL RICE PUDDING

600 ml (1 pint) MILK
1 VANILLA POD
50 g (2 oz) PUDDING RICE
25 g (1 oz) CASTER SUGAR
15 g (1/2 oz) UNSALTED BUTTER

Preheat the oven to 150°C (300°F/Gas mark 2). Butter a 900 ml (1½ pint) pie dish. Heat the milk slowly with the vanilla pod until hand-hot. Cover and leave for 1 hour. Put the rice into the buttered dish with the sugar and butter. Strain the milk over the rice and stir well. Bake, uncovered, for 2 hours, stirring in the first two skins that form, then allowing the pudding to finish cooking undisturbed.   SERVES 4

SOUTHERN RICE PUDDING

This recipe is an American version of the rice pudding, and is influenced by the Mexicans. A similar pudding is popular with the Portuguese who love to add generous quantities of dried fruit, nuts and spices.

225 ml (8 fl oz) WATER
75 g (3 oz) PUDDING RICE
1 VANILLA POD
pinch of SALT
600 ml (1 pint) MILK
2 (size 4) EGGS, BEATEN
75 g (3 oz) SUGAR
1.25 ml (1/4 tsp) GROUND CINNAMON
75 g (3 oz) SEEDLESS RAISINS
FRESHLY GRATED NUTMEG

Preheat the oven to 180°C (350°F/Gas mark 4). Butter a 900 ml (1½ pint) pie dish.

Bring the water to the boil in a saucepan. Add the rice, vanilla pod and salt and simmer very gently for 10 minutes, until all the liquid has been absorbed. Pour in half the milk and simmer for another 10 minutes. Meanwhile, whisk together the remaining milk, the eggs, sugar and cinnamon. Remove the pan from the heat and stir in the egg mixture. Remove the vanilla pod. Pour the rice mixture in to the buttered dish. Stir in the raisins, and sprinkle with nutmeg. Stand the dish in a roasting tin half-filled with hot water. Bake, uncovered, for 1 hour until firm.   SERVES 6

TOP: TRADITIONAL RICE PUDDING   BOTTOM: SOUTHERN RICE PUDDING

RASPBERRY BRÛLÉE

50 g (2 oz) RICE FLOUR
50 g (2 oz) CASTER SUGAR
2.5 ml (1/2 tsp) GROUND CINNAMON
600 ml (1 pint) MILK
225 g (8 oz) FRESH RASPBERRIES
90 ml (6 tbsp) DEMERARA SUGAR

Put the rice flour, caster sugar and cinnamon in a saucepan and gradually stir in the milk. Bring to the boil, stirring. Reduce the heat to very low and cook for 10 minutes, stirring frequently. Carefully stir in the raspberries, then turn into a 20 x 15 cm (8 x 6 inch) ovenproof dish or six individual dishes. Preheat the grill to very hot. Sprinkle the demerara sugar over the rice to completely cover the surface. Place under the grill until the sugar caramelises. Serve immediately.

SERVES 6

PEACH MERINGUE PUDDING

75 g (3 oz) PUDDING RICE
600 ml (1 pint) MILK
150 g (5 oz) CASTER SUGAR
2.5 ml (1/2 tsp) GRATED NUTMEG
2 (size 4) EGGS, SEPARATED
40 ml (8 tsp) RASPBERRY CONSERVE
4 RIPE PEACHES, PEELED, HALVED AND STONED

Preheat the oven to 190°C (375°F/Gas mark 5). Put the rice, milk, 25 g (1 oz) caster sugar, and the nutmeg into a pan. Bring to the boil, then lower the heat and simmer very gently for about 25 minutes, stirring frequently, until the rice is cooked and most of the milk absorbed.

Beat the egg yolks into the rice, then pour into a 1.1 litre (2 pint) soufflé dish. Place a little raspberry conserve in each peach half. Arrange some of the peaches around the inside of the soufflé dish, with the cut sides pressing against the sides of the dish. Place the remaining peaches, jam-side down, on the rice. Whisk the egg whites until stiff. Whisk in half the remaining sugar, then fold in the remainder. Spoon on to the rice. Bake for about 5 minutes. Serve hot, or leave to cool, then chill before serving.

SERVES 8

LEFT: PEACH MERINGUE PUDDING
RIGHT: RASPBERRY BRÛLÉE

Calas Tous Chauds

Calas are rice fritters which were sold in the streets of the French Quarter in New Orleans by women known as Calas women. Their early morning cries of Calas Tous Chauds would bring out the residents for their early morning snack. This recipe needs to be started a day in advance.

125 g (4 oz) PUDDING RICE
900 ml (1½ pint) WATER
2.5 ml (½ tsp) SALT
15 g (½ oz) DRIED YEAST
125 ml (4 fl oz) WARM WATER
50 g (2 oz) SUGAR
3 (size 4) EGGS
5 ml (1 tsp) GRATED LEMON ZEST
1.25 ml (¼ tsp) GRATED NUTMEG
200 g (7 oz) PLAIN FLOUR
OIL FOR FRYING
ICING SUGAR

Sauce
75 g (3 oz) LIGHT SOFT BROWN SUGAR
50 ml (2 fl oz) MAPLE SYRUP
10 ml (2 tsp) WATER
15 g (½ oz) UNSALTED BUTTER
25 g (1 oz) PECANS, CHOPPED

Put the rice, water and salt into a saucepan. Bring to the boil. Cover and simmer for 30 minutes until the rice is very soft. Drain, cool, and mash the rice. Dissolve the yeast in the warm water with 5 ml (1 tsp) of the sugar, according to the packet instructions. Pour the yeast liquid into the rice. Stir well. Cover with a damp tea towel and leave in a warm place overnight.

The next day, beat the eggs with the remaining sugar, the lemon zest, nutmeg and two-thirds of the flour. Add to the rice mixture and beat well. Beat in the remaining flour for 2 minutes. Cover with a damp tea towel and leave to rise in a warm place for 1 hour.

To make the sauce, put the sugar, maple syrup, water and butter into a small saucepan. Heat slowly, stirring, until the sugar has melted. Stir in the chopped pecans, cover, and keep warm over a very low heat. Pour a 2.5 cm (1 inch) layer of oil into a shallow frying pan. Heat to 190°C (375°F). Preheat the oven to 200°C (400°F/Gas mark 6). Carefully spoon four portions of the rice mixture into the oil, and fry for 2 minutes, turning once. Check the temperature of the oil regularly. Drain on paper towels and keep warm in the oven whilst frying the rest. Dust the fritters with icing sugar. Serve hot with the sauce.   MAKES 24

Indian Rice Pudding

Long grain rice can be substituted for basmati rice in this recipe.

4 CARDAMOM PODS
15 g (½ oz) BUTTER
125 g (4 oz) BASMATI WHITE RICE
25 g (1 oz) FLAKED ALMONDS
600 ml (1 pint) MILK
50 g (2 oz) SOFT BROWN SUGAR

Slit the cardamom pods open and remove the seeds. Crush the seeds with a rolling pin. Melt the butter in a saucepan, add the crushed seeds and rice, and cook gently for 1 minute. Add the almonds and milk. Bring to the boil, cover and simmer very gently for 20 minutes, stirring frequently, until the rice is tender and the liquid has been absorbed. Stir in the sugar and serve.   SERVES 4

RIGHT: CALAS TOUS CHAUDS

R-ICE COCONUT CREAM

This is an unusual ice cream studded with the texture of rice which has absorbed the delicate fragrance of jasmine tea. You can substitute long grain rice for jasmine rice in this recipe.

5 ml (1 tsp)	JASMINE TEA LEAVES
125 ml (¼ pint)	BOILING WATER
25 g (1 oz)	JASMINE WHITE RICE
2 (size 3)	EGGS
50 g (2 oz)	CASTER SUGAR
15 ml (1 tbsp)	CORNFLOUR
300 ml (½ pint)	MILK
125 g (4 oz)	CREAMED COCONUT, FINELY CHOPPED
142 ml (¼ pint)	DOUBLE CREAM

To Serve

30 ml (2 tbsp)	DESICCATED COCONUT
	FRESH FRUIT SALAD
	JASMINE TEA

Put the tea leaves into a jug. Pour over the boiling water, and leave to infuse for 5 minutes. Strain the tea into a saucepan. Add the rice and cook as directed on page 14. Cool.

Whisk together the eggs, sugar and cornflour. Heat the milk in a saucepan until almost boiling, then pour over the egg mixture, whisking continuously. Return to the pan and heat gently, stirring, until the custard thickens. Do not boil. Take off the heat and stir in the creamed coconut. Leave to cool.

Put the cold cooked rice and the cream in a food processor, blend until smooth, then stir into the cooled custard. Pour into a 750 ml (1¼ pint) shallow freezer container and freeze for 2 hours. Cover and store.

To serve, remove from the freezer 1½ hours before required. Preheat the grill. Toast the coconut under the grill until golden. Unmould the ice cream and cut into 6-8 portions. Sprinkle with the toasted coconut. Serve with fresh fruit salad and a cup of jasmine tea. SERVES 6-8

CHOCOLATE TREATS

125 g (4 oz)	DARK CHOCOLATE, CHOPPED
125 g (4 oz)	WHITE CHOCOLATE, CHOPPED
50 g (2 oz)	BUTTER OR MARGARINE, CHOPPED
30 ml (2 tbsp)	MAPLE SYRUP
125 g (4 oz)	RICE KRISPIES
50 g (2 oz)	GLACÉ CHERRIES, CHOPPED
115 g (4.06 oz)	PACKET WHITE CHOCOLATE DROPS
115 g (4.06 oz)	PACKET DARK CHOCOLATE DROPS

Melt the chocolates in two separate medium-sized bowls, placed over a saucepan of hot water. Melt the butter or margarine and maple syrup in a small saucepan, then pour half the mixture over the dark chocolate, the remainder over the white chocolate. Stir well, then stir in the rice breakfast cereal and cherries. Cool until just before setting, then stir the white chocolate drops into the dark chocolate mixture and the dark chocolate drops into the white chocolate mixture. Spoon into paper cases. Refrigerate to set.

MAKES APPROXIMATELY 30

TOP: CHOCOLATE TREATS BOTTOM: R-ICE COCONUT CREAM

Spicy Plum Rice Puddings

600 ml (1 pint) MILK
65 g (2½ oz) PUDDING RICE
25 g (1 oz) SUGAR
2.5 ml (½ tsp) GROUND CINNAMON
2 (size 4) EGGS, BEATEN
2-3 PLUMS, STONED AND SLICED
15-20 ml (3-4 tsp) HONEY, WARMED

Preheat the oven to 170°C (325°F/Gas mark 3). Put the milk, rice, sugar and cinnamon into a saucepan. Bring to the boil, cover, and simmer gently for about 25 minutes, stirring occasionally. Cool slightly, then stir in the eggs.

Grease and line bases of six to eight 5.5 cm (2¼ inch) deep dariole moulds or teacups. Arrange some of the sliced plums in the base of each mould, then spoon in the rice pudding. Stand the dishes in a roasting tin half-filled with hot water. Cover each mould com- pletely with oiled foil. Cook in the oven for 50 minutes. Remove the moulds from the tin and leave for about 10 minutes. Turn out on to small plates and spoon over the warm honey.

SERVES 6-8

Lemon Rice Caramel

125 g (4 oz) PUDDING RICE
750 ml (26 fl oz) MILK
142 ml (¼ pint) DOUBLE CREAM
3 (size 4) EGGS, BEATEN
grated zest and juice of 1 LEMON

Caramel
175 g (6 oz) SUGAR
90 ml (6 tbsp) WATER

To make the caramel, put the sugar and water into a small saucepan and heat gently, until the sugar dissolves. Bring to the boil and boil gently, without stirring, until golden. Remove the pan from the heat and allow to darken a little more. Pour into eight 5.5 cm (2¼ inch) deep dariole moulds or cups, or into a 1 litre (1¾ pint) ring mould. Swirl the dishes so that the sides are well coated. Set aside.

Preheat the oven to 170°C (325°F/Gas mark 3). Put the rice and milk into another saucepan. Bring to the boil, cover, and simmer very gently for 25 minutes. Cool slightly then stir in cream, eggs, lemon zest and juice. Spoon the mixture over the caramel and bake for 30 minutes for individual moulds, 1 hour for a large mould, or until firm. Unmould on to plates or a dish immediately. Serve hot or cold.

SERVES 8

LEFT: SPICY PLUM RICE PUDDING   RIGHT: LEMON RICE CARAMEL

INDEX

Acknowledgements
The authors and publisher would like to thank the following:
The US Rice Council, The UK Rice Association and Ente Nazionale Risi; Annabel Carmichael for typing
the original manuscript; and Lesley Scott for contributing some recipe material. Thanks also go to Debbie Boeger for
the California Company recipe and to Laverne Seidenstricker for the Camphouse Trout recipe.

Photography Credits
All photography is credited to Simon Butcher, except the following:
Clint Brown, pages 37 and 73; and Melvin Grey, page 81.